Running the Good Race

BY ANITA BRYANT

Mine Eyes Have Seen the Glory
Amazing Grace
Bless This House

BY ANITA BRYANT AND BOB GREEN

Fishers of Men
Light My Candle
Running the Good Race

Anita Bryant & Bob Green

Running the Good Race

Fleming H. Revell Company
Old Tappan, New Jersey

Scripture quotations in this volume are from the King James Version of the Bible.

Excerpts from "Clean Living May Be the Best Medicine" by Ronald Katulack are reprinted by courtesy of the *Chicago Tribune*.

With Praise to God!
TO our beloved Farfar and Pop
Einar Green
1900–1976

Contents

Running
the
Good Race

Bob

1
Running to Win

"A BOOK ABOUT *running?* Physical fitness?" I must have stared at Anita like she had lost her marbles.

"We wouldn't write about running, exactly," she answered slowly. "More about *winning.* Running the good race means you're running to win—that you really want the prize. So many of us Christians just plug along, puffing away, then run out of steam when we need it most.

"Just like me when I jog," she continued. "When I see that little hill come toward me, I always quit running and begin to walk. I can't face that hill!"

"Hang in there. You'll conquer the hill," I told her. And soon she did.

That little episode occurred nearly two years ago. As Anita perceived parallels between the jogging discipline she thought she hated, and the spiritual discipline she knew she loved, she began to pitch me some challenging questions.

How does a lazy Christian get off the starting line? Is it *too late* for me to run?

How can we help our children develop mental, spiritual, and physical muscle tone?

Can a disciple *detest* discipline?

What happens when I stumble or fall—or quit running? And most important is *do I really want to win the prize? And is our family oriented toward winning?*

"Seek, and ye shall find," Jesus said (Matthew 7:7, Luke 11:9). Meanwhile, as we were seeking, we got all kinds of letters and feedback from readers who encounter the exact same kinds of challenges the Green family faces—a lot of personal stress, too little time, maybe a money shortage, plus the problems of trying to rear kids in our permissive society, or deciding what to do about aging parents—all very real stuff, none of it Mickey Mouse.

Many correspondents confessed that, like Anita had, they seek a healing of the emotions. In *Light My Candle* she shared her breakdown experience very openly which brought us a flood of mail. Christians from every stratum of society thanked Anita for bringing up the subject of emotional problems for discussion. We saw it *needed* some Christian discussion!

Others wrote to me, wanting detailed advice about jogging or diet or sharing their own experiences along those lines.

Anita and I set aside the letters and articles and newspaper clippings. *Running the Good Race* began to take shape in our minds. We knew we would write it for ourselves and our children as much as for anyone else. Meanwhile, of course, we were living the book.

We soon discovered we needed to get much deeper into the Bible in search of some real answers. (It is amazing, the things we had been reading all those years and not seeing!) We started discovering some mind-blowing truths—both in God's holy Word and in God's holy people.

Running the Good Race began to take off. We're in those early laps right now—looking toward a great horizon. We are certainly not winners yet, but are aiming toward the prize. Before we sprint too much farther, however, let's introduce—or update you on—the six members of the Green Family Team.

Anita Bryant, my wife, perhaps is best known today as America's Florida orange juice girl. Florida's Governor Reubin Askew wrote, "People connect orange juice, Florida, and Anita Bryant so much that it becomes difficult to decide which to visit, which to listen to, and which to squeeze!"

All jests aside, Anita's position as spokeswoman for the Florida Citrus Commission is something our family takes pride in. We're all great Florida boosters—and since 1968, when Anita and the Florida Citrus Growers joined forces, Florida and citrus certainly have become synonymous in the minds of the American public.

Long before that of course, Anita Bryant had been solidly established in her multifaceted performing career, including concerts, summer stock, recording, radio, television, and personal appearances of many sorts.

Anita has sung for American servicemen at military posts all over the globe, for presidents and royalty, and for the unsung and often unvisited heroes in veterans hospitals all over the country.

She has represented many of America's topflight industries, civic clubs and political and patriotic organizations, has spoken and testified in song at Billy Graham Crusades, Oral Roberts TV specials, and the "Stars and Stripes Show," and has commentated at our own great Orange

Bowl Parade, Junior Orange Bowl Parade, and Super Bowl extravaganzas here in Miami.

Others know Anita from her appearances at local prayer breakfasts, colleges, or small-town churches—each as important to us as any audience of many millions!

Obviously, I'm proud of my wife. But to me, the Anita Green who is my wife and our children's mommie shines as the real star of my life. She's no temperamental performer, but a woman who loves the Lord and seeks to grow in His grace and favor.

That's the Anita I love best. No other performance she might ever give could surpass what I see each day in Anita Bryant Green—a truly dedicated Christian, my wife, our children's devoted mother, and my prayer partner, tennis partner, and business partner.

Sixteen years of marriage to Anita have deflected me from my own early career in broadcasting into some other exciting enterprises—Bob Green Productions, Inc., for example, and our more recently established Fishers of Men Opportunities, Inc., a Christian talent agency.

Managing Anita's career and coordinating activities with her agent, Dick Shack, a top Miami talent agent, gets more complicated all the time. We're constantly challenged to keep her professional schedule uncomplicated enough to allow our home life to come first—something our four kids and I consider paramount.

Each of our children is presently into physical fitness in a big way. The interesting thing is it was caught—not taught. When they saw their parents' faithfulness about running, the kids on their own decided it must have some value. One by one, they fell in with us.

Bobby, just thirteen, now runs five or six miles a day. He

has shot up taller than his mother and is all long legs and broad shoulders. He's a talented boy, who is always learning something new. We call him our professor-at-large.

Gloria, twelve, said Bobby could be anything he wants to be when he grows up. "He may be president someday," she told me seriously. Gloria always has admired her big brother. Like him, she's a good, natural athlete, and she's running at least four miles a day this summer.

Gloria also is a very feminine little girl. She enjoys cooking and has a real talent for piano and ballet as well.

The twins, Billy and Barbara, are seven and one-half and into sports early because of their big brother and sister. They enjoy swimming, waterskiing, snow skiing, and this summer began to run from one to two miles a day. All of the children are keeping a Jog Log of their own.

Billy is a natural athlete who probably will do well at sports of any type. He's also talented at art. Barbara, who loves to sing or talk your ear off, enjoys ballet and "keeping house"; she likes to help her mother serve refreshments and to work in the kitchen.

This summer the twins discovered Anita's first book, *Mine Eyes Have Seen the Glory,* and read it. We were curious to hear their reaction, but at first they didn't say a word. I guess they think everybody's mommie writes books.

The other day at supper, however, Anita turned to me and called me *Robert.* Barbara suddenly got very interested. "Oh-oh, Daddy," she said. "In the book it says when Mommie calls you *Robert,* it means she's mad at you!"

Billy and Barbara proceeded from there to *Amazing Grace,* Anita's second book, but so far, we haven't received a book report.

We do receive book reports from many, many interested

Christians across America, however, and we really treasure these messages. A friend who, like us, experienced the birth of premature twins wrote:

"When the twins were born and they remained in the hospital, I read *Mine Eyes Have Seen the Glory,* and my faith was strengthened. *Amazing Grace* and *Fishers of Men* both helped me so much to realize the power we have to witness. *Bless This House* changed my attitudes in my marriage, but at a time when I began to question my own faith, *Light My Candle* came. My mother is mentally ill, and we had faced a number of deaths in our family. That book was a godsend. I keep wondering what the Lord is going to have you write next!"

Anita and I always wonder the same thing. Recently we have been coping with super pressures, especially during America's bicentennial year, and with the help of the Lord, handling the whole thing in a totally new way.

The crises continue to come—everything from tripling our work schedule to losing some key staff members, dealing with preadolescent children to a sick and sometimes difficult parent, bearing with a disrupted house while attending to the details and decisions involved in building an addition, and learning, really for the first time, to handle money—all sorts of challenges to better discipline.

We realize it's vitally important that we learn to run so we can win. All our life is a race, God says, and in Isaiah 40:31 He tells us:

> But they that wait upon the Lord shall renew their strength; they shall mount up with wings as eagles; they shall run, and not be weary; and they shall walk, and not faint.

There's a time to mount up with wings, another time to run, and still another time when we must walk and not faint.

Running the Good Race will carry on from where our earlier books left off. From Anita's Jog Log, I copied these notes.

"We Christians, more than anyone else in the world, need to stay fit for combat. This life becomes a battleground at times, and we're told to put on the whole armor of God.

"Most of us would make terrible soldiers because we're in terrible condition. So many of us Christians seem to find the world controlling *us*—instead of realizing that we can overcome the *world!*

"In our household, deciding to get our bodies fit was the beginning of wisdom. One by one we added on other disciplines—increased prayer vitality, a richer family life, more responsibility toward one another, and better self-control."

Another entry I like is where Anita compared the benefits of *jogging* to those of *salvation*. Jogging:

- It's free
- No special facilities needed
- Old and young can do it
- Improves the heart and lungs
- Helps you feel and look better
- Helps you strip away excess fat
- Builds endurance and confidence
- Is something you can do alone or with others

Because this is mostly our story, not everything in this book reflects success. For example, my chapter entitled "Confessions of a Foodaholic" will have to include my recent three-day orgy which began with lunch at a French restaurant and ended with pizza, ice cream, and candy at Gloria's birthday party.

Then there's a rocky stretch of road in Anita's experience called "Confessions of a Spendaholic"—and Anita, like me, will be the first to testify that she has some more roadwork to do with the Lord.

The important thing is He stays in there with us. His Bible instructs and inspires us and remains the only perfect guidebook to use over the long haul. And if we should stumble and fall, Jesus picks us up every time.

As Paul wrote in 1 Corinthians 9:24–27:

> Know ye not that they which run in a race run all, but one receiveth the prize? So run, that ye may obtain.
>
> And every man that striveth for the mastery is temperate in all things. Now they do it to obtain a corruptible crown; but we an incorruptible;
>
> I therefore so run, not as uncertainly; so fight I, not as one that beateth the air:
>
> But I keep under my body, and bring it into subjection: lest that by any means, when I have preached to others, I myself should be a castaway.

Amen!

I close with a response to Anita's question about being too old to learn to run. (And I hope you realize we mean *run* figuratively.)

A newspaper clipping tells about a sixty-nine-year-old lady who has climbed a Sierra Nevada peak fourteen times. She started climbing at about age sixty-four.

Well, it shows how much more people can do than they think they can do. For the Christian, the lesson is that God will take us at any point and teach us new things—how to run, how to climb, or how to "Be still, and know that I am God" (Psalms 46:10).

He's not too busy to help us go "from glory to glory" (2 Corinthians 3:18), as Paul describes it. Throughout the following pages we'll be challenging you to join the Green Team in our running—whether it be physical, mental, or spiritual.

We'll be running the good race—and running to win!

2

Good Morning, God!

LIKE ANY OTHER housewife with four young children, I had no intention of rising at six A.M. and running a mile. Who needs it?

But one January day in 1975 in a weak moment I yielded to Bob's steady propaganda and nagging, and I tried running the good race. That fifteen-minute *run* (half of it walking) literally changed my life.

Today I'm a full-fledged fan of aerobic exercise. I beat the drums for running, biking, swimming, fast walking, jumping rope, or any other means whereby you exert your heart, lung, and circulatory system.

The running I thought I hated literally revolutionized my life. Today I possess twice the energy I had two years ago, though my work load is three times heavier. My skin looks good; tension headaches have lessened; digestive problems are a thing of the past; and amazingly, the arthritis that has plagued me for years seems to be on its way out. Hallelujah!

But I'm getting ahead of my story. Two years ago, every time Bob tried to get me to join his jogging program, I had a bunch of reasons not to. "How can any mother of four kids need to run?" I challenged him. "I don't have a weight problem, I do have this big house to keep up with, and anyhow, my ballet and tennis lessons keep me in shape."

I figured I had absolutely no reason to run, but I had a big reason not to: *I loathed the whole idea!* Jogging (the physical fitness method Bob chose) appealed to me about as much as cold fried eggs. Ugh!

Grandma Berry used to say confession is good for the soul; so here goes. The truth is when Bob first started running, it made me very angry. Jogging meant he was away from the breakfast table, away from the kids and me first thing in the morning, missing family devotions, and copping out in general.

I didn't like it a bit. I thought he had become a fanatic. What's more, Bob seemed so totally selfish and absorbed in his exercise program that I resented it for a long, long time. That was unfair of me.

Soon after he turned forty, Bob and I were really shook when Bob experienced symptoms of what the doctors at first believed was a serious heart condition. It really scared us. When it turned out to be a false alarm, Bob listened to his doctors' advice and undertook to get his body in shape. He lost forty pounds and began the physical fitness program he intends to follow the rest of his life.

All very good, except I refused to accept how vitally important it was for him to put himself immediately into the best possible physical condition. Bob realized halfway measures would never do it, but I could only see the drastic changes taking place in our household routine—and I hated the changes.

So we had a total lack of communication about the whole thing. So far as I was concerned, *jogging* was a dirty word.

Meanwhile, I tried to hide those feelings, pitying myself for having to put up with Bob's lack of cooperation. I thought of myself as patient and long-suffering when really I was full of anger and hostility.

As the weeks and months wore on, my resentment (which I didn't always bother to hide) increased. The only thing I could do about the situation was pray that something would change—and what do you know, the Lord began to change my attitudes!

Bob was changing in a lot of ways, too. He could take stress so much better, for example. His disposition improved a lot as he began to siphon off some of his frustrations through regular exercise. And certainly I had to admit I could see steady improvement in such things as weight loss and muscle tone. Moreover, he was feeling good—and feeling good about himself.

But what mattered most to me was that the changes I was seeing in Bob's physical body and emotional structure provided a powerful testimony to Christ's ability to help my husband discipline himself. Day in and day out, this spoke to me.

Funny thing, for a long time Bob nagged me about jogging until I became very defiant about the nagging. His words totally turned me off, but the discipline and perseverance he displayed turned me on. I heard the things he said as challenging and antagonistic, but the example he showed was superconvincing.

In the end his example, not his words, influenced me profoundly. (Christians, there's a big lesson there.) And meanwhile, as he continued to improve through disciplined exercise, my own physical condition became less and less to brag about. I was experiencing a lot of work-related tensions which came out in my physical body.

Show business is not exactly restful. Young as I was, some distressing symptoms of aging were beginning to show up: allergies, arthritis, circulatory problems, and similar stress signals. I was always working, always tired, and always bothered with some sort of minor physical ailment.

That's how the Lord continued to nudge me. I had sense enough to know there was no way I was going to wake up one morning feeling perfectly grand either. To be honest, I usually dragged out of bed in the morning. It had been a long time since I felt really good.

(I once heard a preacher say there are two ways to wake up in the morning. One is "Good morning, God!" The other is "Good God, it's morning!")

Eventually a case of old-fashioned flu put me in bed for a week. While I lay there, tired, worn out, and fed up, the Lord convinced me of the fact that I am responsible for taking care of my body, and I *wasn't* taking good care of it. I knew I could continue to feel sorry for myself and keep on going to pot, or I could pick myself up and give the whole thing to the Lord.

I also knew I didn't have the self-discipline even to get started exercising. I hated the thought. So I made a covenant with the Lord: I'd get up every morning and He could make me run! I'd put on jogging clothes and go outdoors, and He could take it from there.

Would you believe He did?

The first morning was a tremendously humbling experience. Bob had measured off the one-mile point; so I took off, expecting to do it like nothing. What happened really unnerved me; huffing, puffing, with pain in my neck and chest (not used to taking in so much oxygen), half-walking, and half-running, I barely managed to complete my mile and returned to the house filled with self-disgust.

"Don't worry about it," Bob advised. "Did you know that very few adults are capable of running a mile?"

"I didn't know that," I replied, "but even if it's true, I sure thought *I* could!" (Anyone over thirty who begins a strenuous exercise program should first get the okay from his doctor. The E-K-G under-stress test should be included in the checkup.)

I learned a long time ago to set a definite time in my day to be with the Lord, and I also know myself well enough to set a definite time for exercise. If I postpone either, it's likely to go undone that day. Satan loves to intervene.

If I don't schedule things, I find they don't get done. I write everything down and assign myself a time to do it. Marabel Morgan, in her Total Woman classes, advocates a $25,000 Plan for writing everything down. I told Marabel I've always had a $100,000 Plan. I have learned it's possible to have my six A.M. devotions, get the kids fed and off to school, run, shower, and eat breakfast before 8:30 A.M.

That first week or so, while you're building up muscles, you discover a few little aches and pains and perhaps some tiredness, but *on the very first day I felt better.* You feel relaxed and energetic. That increased oxygen intake brings immediate new life into your system.

Isn't that a parallel to the spiritual life—that the more you give out to God, the more obedient you become, and the more He fills you? It's exactly the same with an exercise discipline; the more you do, the more extra things you find yourself able to accomplish. You won't believe it until you have tried it!

It's incredible. Long before I began jogging, I understood the truth that the more you take on for the Lord—including hard work, stresses, and trials—the more He will help you do and the more you realize that afflictions somehow bounce off you.

But the key word is commitment. If you want to become physically fit, feel good, look your best, and take care of the temple where God dwells, you must make up your mind to do it. When you accept Christ into your life or when you enter into marriage, you don't place a time limit on the transaction or think of falling away. It's like that; it's a commitment.

I still don't always like running, but I sure like myself after I run! It reminds me of a statement by C. S. Lovett: "When I am getting the worst of it, God is making the most of it, to see that I get the best of it."

In order for us to be holy, so many Christians think we should keep our heads and our eyes up in the clouds. We're so heavenly minded that we're no earthly good.

The truth is the word *holy* is kin to the words *whole* and *healthy*. Good health in our spirit, soul, and body is God's intention for us. I wonder what kind of letter the Apostle Paul would write to us flabby Americans today concerning holiness?

I'm praying the Holy Spirit will move the minds and hearts of people as they read this book because I believe God's ideal of wholeness for us is something we neglect. We get out there and try to win souls, but we forget to disciple.

God told us to disciple; He says, "Let the redeemed of the Lord say so" (Psalms 107:2).

We all tend to follow strong, mature, and attractive people. Jesus must have been physically attractive, when you consider all the hard labor and all the walking he did. He had the muscular, healthy physical appearance that drew other rugged men to Him. Sedentary Christians can't have the dynamic power and stamina or display the sheer joy of living that God wants us to enjoy.

Aerobic exercise by now has become as vitally important to me as my skin and hair care, vitamin C from Florida orange juice, additional vitamins, good food, and sleep. At some point each one of us must decide whether or not we intend to become a healthy and physically fit human being. We need to make a commitment, and we need to go about it properly. (Later in the book, Bob has some terrific tips on how to get into aerobics, which so many doctors advocate as the best route to fitness, no matter what your age category.)

It is important too that we practice exercise just as faithfully as we practice prayer. The effect jogging has had on Bob inspired Dr. Stanley Jonas (our family doctor) and his wife to begin jogging. But they took it one step farther and now jog every day of their lives, no matter where they are, including jogging all over Europe. Their example encouraged Bob and me to hit the trail in whatever cities we find ourselves, whether we run along a beautiful beach at Cape Canaveral, through the desert near Pasco, Washington, or take a few laps around a Holiday Inn parking lot. Looking back, it seems incredible that I ever resented Bob's early morning jogging.

Sometimes we gals find ourselves tempted to skip a day for cosmetic reasons, but I've found a trick that protects my hair. I put it up in pin curls, tie a scarf around my head, and after my shower I find the dampness from running and bathing actually helps set my hair. We'll always find a way to do the things we want and mean to do.

As Bob and I travel about the country, we're noticing more and more people out jogging in the early morning or early evening. It feels so great to get that blood circulating!

In fact, just as the blood of Jesus cleanses the world, so does our blood cleanse our own bodies. But while the Bible emphasizes that we're to take care of our bodies, it's important to realize that the bodies themselves—without God's spirit—are as lifeless as anything that is dead. There's no real life there, because only the indwelling Spirit of Christ gives us life. As Paul said, ". . . know ye not that your body is the temple of the Holy Ghost" (1 Corinthians 6:19).

That's why I begin each morning by first building up my spiritual defenses. My early devotions provide the will and desire and fortitude to undertake the physical disciplines—and that completes the circle.

Once you work hard to get that blood flowing (and I'm not talking about housework) the increased amount of oxygen in your bloodstream begins to take effect. The brain works better. You discover new, quick mental responses, good idea power.

The increased blood circulation cleanses the body of impurities. You feel good. I enjoy twice my former energy and endurance, and I am still amazed to discover I can do three appearances a day with breath and energy to spare.

And that is my deepest heart's desire, to learn more and

more how to do everything as unto the Lord. God is the Author of Life; He is Life.

God is sovereign in His universe. Not only did He create all things, but He is the one who manages all things and holds all things together (*see* Colossians 1:16–17).

He has "appointed a day, in which he will judge the world in righteousness" (Acts 17:31), but He loves each one of us (*see* John 3:16); He has communicated Himself to us (*see* Hebrews 1:1–2), and He is "not willing that any should perish, but that all should come to repentance" (2 Peter 3:9).

We can trust in God and find Him to be real and personal. He can become to each of us just what He is—our heavenly Father! And when we do relate to God in the biblical way, we cleanse our conscience from various corruptions (*see* Hebrews 9:14, 10:22). We establish a relationship with the perfect Parent through His grace in Jesus Christ.

For me, that relationship begins early in the morning. First, it starts with devotions, for in Proverbs 8:17 God says: "I love them that love me; and those that seek me early shall find me."

Next comes the discipline of fitness, for as Paul wrote in Romans 12:1: "I beseech you therefore, brethren, by the mercies of God, that ye present your bodies a living sacrifice, holy, acceptable unto God, which is your reasonable service."

It's a fantastic way to start the day—loving and praising and serving the Lord. Even a slow starter can learn to become a morning person—a *happy* morning person, would you believe!—maybe even the first on the block to jog down the street with his whole self singing "Good morning, God!"

Anita

3
One Day at a Time

DO YOU KEEP A DIARY? When I began my exercise discipline all those months ago, I followed Bob's example and began a Jog Log. He records the date, time, distance run, weather conditions, and other facts, always noting any special reactions or improvements. Bob says keeping a log prevents boredom from setting in.

He's right. It's fun to look back over the months and see what the Lord is doing. For example, the first time I tried to run a mile I probably walked more than I ran. That went on for a while, but in a surprisingly short time, I was running pretty fast.

One evening after returning from a booking, Bob reminded me that we hadn't had a chance to run that morning and said, "Why don't we go out now?"

"I'm too tired," I told him.

"Sometimes when you think you're too tired that's the very time you run the best and when it's the best for you," he replied.

Since I felt too tired to argue with him, we ran. That turned out to be the first time I ran my mile without walking any part of it in twelve minutes, and it made me so excited.

In fact, looking back, that's when I knew I was hooked on jogging!

I had started out tired, relaxed, and not caring what happened—which is exactly why it turned out so well. Praise the Lord! How absurd to go from feeling totally blah to totally exhilarated, from tired and dispirited to excited and proud, in twelve short minutes.

We can obtain the same results spiritually. We run the best spiritual race when we are too tired to continue ourselves and are willing to let the Lord take over.

If you could peek into my Jog Log, you'd laugh. For one thing, I titled it *Anita's Laments* and proceeded to pour out my praises and complaints in big, illegible scrawls. Though my writings will never compete with the Psalms of David, I'll share some bits with you.

One day at a time. Lord, I get so discouraged when I think ahead to how many aerobic points I'm shooting for. It's important to have a goal, but *don't let the goal have me*.

Lord God, it's so tough doing that extra mile or even going that first mile—but then I think how great I'll feel later, knowing I've gotten first things first out of the way! Faithfulness can only happen one day at a time.

Never look back, or you'll lose your stride. Just think of the finish line and the blessings of being a whole person. It doesn't please God for us to neglect the temple He gave us to use during this lifetime. He expects me to keep it in tip-top shape and perfect running condition. He wants us to get up early and prepare ourselves in mind, body, and spirit!

I counted my steps as I ran, and there were approximately one thousand (left and right) in the mile. It was terrible to keep count, as my mind wandered. Also, being preoccupied with counting steps slowed down my pace, and I wasn't looking to the goal. Bob told me that's not good for runners, that we're supposed to look to the horizon instead of counting each individual footfall. So, spiritually speaking, take it *one day at a time* and look to the Horizon, *Jesus,* but don't get so hung up on counting every step.

The world is watching! Often I imagine there are spectators lining the street as I jog. Some are saying, "She'll never make it." Others, fellow believers, are cheering me on. But a few onlookers are brutally cruel and throw litter at me, or—worse still—curse me!

Some believers who never have run are the most critical and judgmental—and I dislike them most of all.

If I look at the spectators or relate to them (except the positive ones who help keep my courage high), I may falter, slow down, stumble, or even stop. It's imperative for the runner to keep his thoughts centered on running and his eyes fixed on the horizon.

Just so, the Christian must run the good race for Christ. We must continue to run even though we fumble and falter (sin) or even stop completely at times. Should we stumble, however, Jesus will pick us up *every time.*

Eventually we can run and not be weary. We're weak, but yet have great potential strength. We're willing to be willing. Letting the mind of Christ be in us and placing the Holy Spirit in full control over our emotions, we gradually learn to keep our eyes on the Horizon which is Jesus. One day at a time!

My goal in life is to know God Himself. Not peace or joy, not even blessings, but Himself. My God!

Funny, I kept saying that runners should look to the Horizon when they run, and I believed it. Still, I never really applied it in my own life until today.

It's amazing how different everything was. The run did not feel burdensome. I saw the same things along my path, but they were not as important as before. Even the dogs didn't matter! Before today, each dog was friend or foe. Today for the first time I actually felt exaltation—*almost a joy*—in running.

Always when I'm not running well, I ask Jesus to help me, and He's with me before, during, and after—*always,* whether or not it's a good run. But today was different. Jesus showed me how the physical *can* work in His plan for our lives. We have a choice; we can wallow in sluggishness or get up and run to unknown goals for our own whole and holy well-being and for the glory of God.

I confess there's another reason I ran better today, too. For two weeks I've been on a mild muscle relaxant. I've had bad pain in my neck, shoulders, arms, knee joints, and even in my big toe. All this started more than a year ago.

Part of the pain is due to arthritis, part is just plain tense muscles, and I tried heat and various other home remedies before resorting to Valium.

Lord, just a tiny fourth of a gram does the job for me, but I found myself taking a whole gram at night—sometimes for pain, but really for no reason at all except that it gradually became habit. It's such a small amount, Lord. It would hardly affect most people at all, but for me, during the day it took away a tinge of my soul control—control of my will, intellect, and emotions—which led to my having some small arguments with Bob, or snapping at the children.

Of course that caused more muscle tension and more need for Valium. Anyhow, I never liked the effect Valium had on me, though every time I told my neurologist about the pain, I rationalized that such a small amount certainly couldn't hurt anything!

Besides, it was very damp and rainy this summer. The medicine was intended to help out until the weather improved. Of course God uses doctors and beneficial drugs to help start healing processes in our body, but so many of America's and the world's illnesses today are self-manufactured to escape life's daily frustrations.

Even Christians resort to pills and alcohol when what they really need is Christ—and now I see how easily this can happen!

What to do when you stumble? Let Jesus Christ pick you up again—and resume the race *immediately*. Lord, how I treasured that time I spent with You alone in the kitchen, the night I decided to throw away the *harmless* pills.

Do you know what, Lord? That's why I could look to
the Horizon today—could see so much clearer—and could
praise Your holy name!

Tribulations. Oswald Chambers wrote that "God will
get our attention through trials and tribulations." Sometimes this is His way of teaching us faith in a particular
area of life. Or sometimes God permits tribulation because
we *are* faithful, Chambers suggests, to allow us to really
know God in His three Persons.

Heavy! This is something no person outside the faith
could understand. Even Christians tend to misinterpret
this kind of attention from God. But the Spirit-filled
believer considers any of God's lessons a blessing.

We must learn to recognize the presence of God in all
things and to praise God *in* and *for* all circumstances.
Even as we run or falter or stumble, He is faithful in preparing us to receive an eternal crown.

Bob

4

Christian Example

IT'S INTERESTING how often the Bible speaks of setting a Christian example. Take a household like ours. With four kids growing up fast, you really have to think about the image you set before them. This preadolescence bit challenges a parent all the way. They test you constantly.

God makes it clear in His word that the husband and father is expected to minister to the needs of every person in his house. The man must oversee the mental, spiritual, and physical welfare of each family member.

Who's equipped for such heavy responsibility? We're not perfect, of course, but just sinners who have to lean on the Lord—which is the whole idea. God wants families to depend on their head and the man to depend on Him.

Meanwhile, your kids look up to you. They watch you like a hawk, and you are their model, for better or worse, from the moment they're old enough to observe.

My decision to jog illustrates how this follow-the-leader works. The way it turned out taught me a great lesson about hanging in there with what the Lord expects and about leading your family by example more than by instructions.

I admit, at first it felt pretty lonely, getting up early and running down the street dressed like a creature from outer space and competing with myself and the dogs every day.

Anita never responded to my invitations to come jog with me, but eventually—more than a year later—she succumbed to my persistency. It was not what I told her, but what she saw me do. And when Anita finally took up the habit that was doing such good things for me, one by one the rest of the family simply fell in with what we were doing.

Bobby was pretty cute about it. He came to me last spring and said, "Dad, last summer you left it up to me whether or not I wanted to run. This summer, please don't give me a choice. Make me run, and punish me if I get lazy and don't do it."

That might sound surprising, but it demonstrates two things: (1) kids want to see you set high standards, and (2) they want you to help discipline them toward worthwhile goals.

The Bible tells us to "Train up a child in the way he should go," (Proverbs 22:6), and God also says that "he that loveth him [his son] chasteneth him" (Proverbs 13:24). When you chasten a child in love, it's surprising how much they invariably love you for it.

Did you ever have a kid cut up to the point that he or she actually seemed to beg for a spanking? And when you maybe had to spank him unwillingly, boy, it cleared the air like magic!

Far better than punishment, of course, is setting right examples in our home, in work habits, worship, and good character—the whole bit. In Ephesians 6:4 Paul says, "And ye fathers, provoke not your children to wrath: but bring them up in the nurture and admonition of the Lord." This strongly suggests that God wants children reared by godly example instead of heavy authoritarian methods and constant punishment.

The great thing about kids is the way they so often spot the inconsistencies and hypocrisies in us adults. In fact, some of us grown-ups who profess Christ should take a good look at ourselves.

At churches all over the country we see great Christian ladies who don't smoke, don't drink, don't wear cosmetics—you name it, they don't do it—but they are obese.

They may go out and knock on doors, witness, and do everything good Christians are supposed to do, but what kind of example do they set? In effect they are saying to the non-Christian, "Hey, look at me. I'm following the rules and regulations of Christian behavior to the letter. I wouldn't drink, wear makeup, dance, or do any of those numbers, but I do weigh two hundred pounds." It's ridiculous.

To speak even more bluntly, there's something very hypocritical about seeing an overweight preacher get up in the pulpit, slam his fist on the Bible, and put down drinking and smoking. His overweight amounts to the same thing he condemns—an abuse of the temple of the Holy Spirit.

A deacon said, "I refuse to let my son wear his hair long." Meanwhile, the son weighs in at 145 pounds and is in superb physical condition, while the father weighs in at 225 pounds and remains in excellent shape to have a heart attack. But he's more concerned with length of hair than length of life.

It's really important for Christians not to be hypocrites. We put ourselves up for ridicule from certain non-Christians who examine us through a microscope. They look for that chink in the armor, that imperfection they can seize on.

As someone said, "What you do speaks so loudly that I can't hear what you say." When Jesus denounced certain people for hypocrisy, he compared them to "whitewashed tombs, full of dead men's bones" ((*see* Matthew 23:27). He couldn't stand the type of religious fraud who said all the right words, but had about as much godliness as you'd find in dead bones.

Watching the XXI Olympic games in Montreal this summer provided our kids with some fantastic examples of Christian winners. Our four all seemed to gravitate toward the TV set, more keenly interested than I'd dreamed they'd be, mainly because for the first time every one of them is into sports in a big way, and they appreciate the discipline and sacrifice sports require.

So here were some of the world's top athletes with the eyes of the world upon them, professing Jesus Christ to the world! It thrilled my heart for our kids to see this happen and to hear these testimonies from the lips of the people they find most interesting and admire so much at this stage of their lives.

We appreciated John Naber, the gold medal swimmer who set a new world record in the 100-meter backstroke. The performance thrilled us, but his giving Jesus the credit *really* excited the whole family.

On the other hand, Madeline Manning Jackson, the Olympic gold medalist of the 1968 games in Mexico City, didn't win this time. She ran what she called "the worst race of my life"; yet she still could praise God and testify that He is all that really matters. What an example of Christian victory in defeat!

Incidentally, the twenty-eight-year-old Madeline Jackson recorded a gospel album titled *Running for Jesus* as she prepared for the 1976 games. Sounds like a winner to me. But one of the most unforgettable testimonies to come out of the 1976 Olympics came from Mrs. Kay Spinks, mother of Leon and Mike Spinks, the first Olympic boxing brothers who are gold medal winners. "I didn't raise them to fight, and I kept praying the Lord would stop their fighting, but He didn't," Mrs. Spinks said. "And since He didn't, I feel sure my boys are meant to go to Montreal and win. God wants His people to win."

They did win, as you know. In fact, the U.S. boxing team, which displayed a powerful faith in God and which often prayed together and for one another, dominated Olympic boxing, bringing home five gold medals and winning thirty-five of forty-one fights.

It's great when we parents can share these moments with our children, can watch their reactions to heroic personalities who also reflect Christ, and can hear what the kids have to say about the testimonies.

In fact, we need to be aware of every sort of example our children are exposed to. Christians need to tune in to what's going on in the world today. The public has a tendency to believe much of what they read in the newspaper or hear on radio or television, then accept it as fact—whether or not it really is.

It's especially critical that parents know what their children listen to on the radio and records. Music today, especially on the rhythm and blues stations, is about 80 percent suggestive or just blatant filth. There's no way the average parent can keep up with current phrases and words that carry double meanings. Do you know all the different words that mean *sex* and *dope* today? The kids listening to our radio stations know. There's a totally new dictionary for these expressions, rather like the CB radio language. It's an in thing, and most parents aren't one bit hip.

This music is appealing. It's very sensuous and it turns you on. I wish there were some way to convince more parents how hard it is to find good music in any category these days—rock, jazz, or country and western—that kids can listen to without being adversely influenced.

What can parents do? When you approach the federal government, which monitors all American radio stations, you're told that banning such records amounts to censorship. Therefore, if we don't want our kids to fill their minds with garbage, we have to make sure we know what they're listening to. It's not easy. We as Christians must alert the sponsors that keep these shows on radio and television that we do not watch or allow our children to watch these shows, and as a result, we do not buy the products that sponsor them.

Another way American parents obviously fail to come through for our youngsters is reflected in these statistics on alcoholism.

Some 450,000 kids between ten and nineteen are alcoholics according to the spring, 1976 edition of *The American Issue* by the American Council on Alcohol Problems.

One-third of all American high school students get drunk every month.

Three out of every four American high school students drink at one time or another.

These are scary statistics because they reflect the lack of parental awareness. We parents must be aware of present-day alcohol problems, drug problems, and also the present-day lack of physical fitness among our youth. We who are Christians can't just be concerned for the boys and girls raised in our own homes, but we must remember the others out there who don't get any kind of a break in life.

Through consistent example, we need to try to raise Christ's standards high for our sons and daughters to *see,* not just hear about.

Anita and I, as we go along, bring to our kids' attention anything challenging or inspirational we happen to read that could stimulate conversation with them concerning moral values.

Bobby liked a Christian Athlete Pledge I discovered in a little publication called *The Total Release Decycler* put out by the Institute for Athletic Perfection. Actually, whether you're an athlete or not, this would be a great pledge to adopt.

In every athletic situation, whether practice or actual competition, I will dedicate myself to give a total release of all that I am, mentally, emotionally, and physically; to become just like Jesus. I will determine to conduct myself in a way that will please the Lord, rather than gain any recognition from men.

Another quote which Bobby liked was: "You should pursue the goal of conforming to the image of Jesus Christ in your athletic competition by fixing your mind on His attitudes instead of your own natural attitudes."

How does a Christian man—husband, father, citizen, church leader, and businessman—learn how to set Christ's example before others? We need to get into the Bible. We need to get on our knees more often. We need to realize how much the kids model after us, how much our wives look to us, and how much our example matters.

I like the Book of Proverbs; it's a great book on child rearing. Ephesians 5:22–33 and Ephesians 6:1–4 explains God's desires for all family relationships.

But it's in Ephesians 4:31–32 that any Christian among us can find a superheavy example of how to live out our lives before others.

> Let all bitterness, and wrath, and anger, and clamour, and evil speaking, be put away from you, with all malice:
> And be ye kind one to another, tenderhearted, forgiving one another, even as God for Christ's sake hath forgiven you.

The father who sets that example will bring up the right kind of sons and daughters, I have to believe. With the help of God, that's what we mean to do.

Anita

5

The Submission Battle

"SUBMISSION? Baloney! Who does *he* think he . . . *mutter . . . grumble . . . storm. . . .*"

Sound familiar, girls? Be honest!

For years I thought *submission* meant doing what *he* wants instead of what *I* want, and the more Christian teaching and preaching on the subject I encountered, the more depressed I felt.

Much has been preached on "Wives, submit yourselves unto your own husbands, as unto the Lord," (Ephesians 5:22), but much less, it seems, on Ephesians 5:25: "Husbands, love your wives, even as Christ also loved the church, and gave himself for it."

So what happens? When you separate one part of a Bible text from the rest, wrong emphasis can result. Frankly, I think many Christian women today trip over the whole idea of submission. I know I have.

To submit means to "throw yourself under" according to the dictionary. It's not something anyone can make me do; it must be voluntary on my part.

Beyond that, submission isn't just a woman's problem. It's a *people* problem. Man, woman, or child, each one of us discovers submission is the only avenue by which we can reach the presence of God.

The Bible abounds with submission stories. Think of Abraham, journeying up Mount Moriah, preparing to sacrifice Isaac, his only son. Or remember David, who had sinned greatly, returning to God and crying, "Restore unto me the joy of thy salvation" (Psalms 51:12).

Job, beset with trials, refused to curse God but instead submitted, saying, "Though he slay me, yet will I trust in him" (Job 13:15). That once-proud intellectual, the apostle Paul, became someone who could humble himself and say, "I have become all things to all men, so that by all means I might be able to win some to Christ" (*see* 1 Corinthians 9:22). And above all, there's the unforgettable example of our Lord Himself, saying to His Father, ". . . nevertheless not as I will, but as thou wilt" (Matthew 26:39).

To comply with God's plan requires submission on my part. The Bible is filled with stories like these, each an act of throwing oneself under God's perfect will in perfect trust. That's what it means to submit.

Someone once asked me what advice I would give to the person whose marriage isn't making it. Well, I don't advise anyone. I can only share what God has done in this home and with our particular group of imperfect people. All any wife can be responsible for—and this should be her first priority—is her own relationship to Jesus Christ. Next, the Bible says she is to submit herself to her husband in that very same way.

Heavy. It takes *submission* to God, in every area of my life, for me to know what He wants for me. But inasmuch as I submit to Him, then can He reveal Himself to me and bring me into a right relationship to husband, children, neighbor, and down the line.

What about the woman who says, "How can I submit to my husband? I'm the only one in this house who honors the Lord or even wants to."

It makes a woman's heart sink to think of coming under submission to such a man, and to tell the truth, it may take years before God has His way with the man. But in the process, I'm convinced, God will teach her something if she determines to practice submission, "as unto the Lord" no matter how bad the situation may be.

In America today, the more usual course is for the woman to choose divorce instead of submission. She says why should I throw my life away? Why sit here and take it? But the Bible says "With God all things are possible" (Matthew 19:26).

Every few days my mail brings verification of this. I hear from girls who have endured very terrible marital situations and all sorts of abuse but who kept the faith, and God brought them through.

However, the majority in that situation today go through divorce. They don't realize the consequences are fully as far-reaching as if they stayed in the marriage—not just for the partners involved, but for the children and for society at large. Sticking it out, no matter how long it takes, surely will prove that God can and will change people and change situations.

Bob and I can witness to that. Married sixteen years and grateful parents of four precious children, we've been blessed beyond the power of words to express. But within those years of what we consider better-than-average marriage and despite our love for those kids and for one another, our marriage, more than once, has met—and survived —some serious assaults.

Let's speak plainly. Satan is running rampant throughout the world these days, and even Christian homes appear vulnerable to his attacks. Ours has been no exception. Bob and I know, from soul-shattering experience, that Satan would love to tear us down—and only as we will rely on the Lord and resort to Him *daily,* can we absolutely count on His divine protection.

Praise the Lord! Today's world offers too many stresses, temptations, bad examples, and every sort of assault of the devil for anyone to assume he is immune to attack. The place for Christian men and women, husbands and wives, fathers and mothers, is on our knees before God. Daily. And some days, even hourly.

In his letter to the Ephesians 6:11–12, Paul instructs them:

> Put on the whole armour of God, that ye may be able to stand against the wiles of the devil.
>
> For we wrestle not against flesh and blood, but against principalities, against powers, against the rulers of the darkness of this world, against spiritual wickedness in high places.

Doesn't that draw a perfect picture of today's world? But cheer up, Christians. God's word gives us ample instructions for "putting on the armour." Bob and I, like many other Christian couples, can testify that God still can and *will* protect the marriage of two people who seek His face daily, read His word daily, and submit themselves to the will of God and to one another.

Sometimes life crowds in so terribly and Satan's assaults come so thick and fast that you don't have anything left to give one another. You don't feel love. You don't feel anything at all except exhaustion.

Maybe you've come to a marital crossroads where you think you've cried every tear, prayed every prayer, hoped every hope—and now there's nothing left. At that point, if you will still cry, still pray, and still hope—that's submission. And no matter what you *think* or what you *feel,* God answers prayers.

The act of submission is something that happens between equals, something that happens by choice. In marriage, submission should be offered by the woman first. That is scriptural. Also I believe, after reading Genesis, that the woman's will often is stronger than the man's.

Only after the woman submits to the man, can the man really love her as he loves his own body and give himself to her as Christ gave Himself for the church. Marriage is a picture of submission to God for the world.

Despite all the good words, many of us women have to fight a daily battle about the submission question. It does not come naturally, and I suspect it never will.

But the battle must be fought, day by day, hour by hour, on the battlefront of marriage and in the home. Once home and marriage are torn down, America is gone. God's picture of the plan of salvation and what it is to have union with Him—that's what is at stake.

Marriage is that picture, the picture of God and man being one, in the flesh.

The main problem about submitting to our husbands is that we look to how weak they are. It's easy to spot their negative traits and the ways they are unworthy to be heads of our households. But who is worthy, except Jesus?

We gals get disgusted and disappointed because our man fails to be perfect. We dwell for a while on those ways he's not even as strong, or mature, or unselfish, or right, as we are. Then we allow ourselves to become frustrated, disappointed, or even enraged and tell ourselves he's not worthy of our submission after all.

So what? Does the Bible promise he will be worthy? Once we submit by obedience, *as unto the Lord*—which is the only way—then with God's help, that man does become stronger. This is God's holy plan, and it pleases Him when we submit. And girls, we don't need to tell ourselves that *our* husband is different and submitting to him won't work. You just go ahead and submit to him *as unto the Lord,* and then it becomes God's business to strengthen and straighten out that man.

As I said, submission doesn't just come naturally. But we soon learn that when we do submit to God first, we find perfect freedom. "Where the Spirit of the Lord is, there is liberty" (2 Corinthians 3:17). There's a strength and a power that never was available before. God made us. He supplies everything. He is the real thing, and the devil can only supply a great-looking imitation.

The truth is we all cringe at the idea of "throwing ourselves under." We want to retain full rights to ourselves; yet Jesus Christ set us the perfect example. He could have called forth legions of angels, could have come down off that cross; yet He chose to submit to the will of His father.

He told us we must take up our cross daily and follow Him. What glorious submission!

But that always has been the bitter battle within every Christian. Nobody wants to take up that cross to crucify *SELF*.

One thing about crucifying *self*—as difficult as it may be—is that later you can share this self-knowledge with other people. I shared this with several of the gals who worked for me, including Kim Russell, who was not only my secretary but also an Anita Bryant Singer.

Kim had *self* on the high and mighty seat. One day I was finally fed up with her grumbling and told her to get on her knees, to name the things in her life that were *self*-dominated, and to confess her selfishness to God. At first she said she couldn't, but finally she did. Since then, *wonderful* is her favorite word. Her confession really made a change in her life.

In *Light My Candle,* the book Bob and I wrote two years ago, I told of when he took me to a famous Christian psychological clinic, the Narramore Christian Foundation in Rosemead, California. A combination of things—grief, family stress, overwork, and physical illness—brought Anita Bryant to the end of her emotional rope. I thought I was losing my mind. Bob recognized that I needed a healing in my emotions, and he immediately took me to California to seek rest, Christian counsel, and therapy.

Talk about submission! As we flew towards California, I made the statement that I wouldn't be coming back—and *I* didn't.

That emotional breakup was my personal crucifixion experience, the nailing of *self* to the cross. I thought it was the

very worst thing that could happen. It terrified me. But
while it was terrible, in a sense, the important thing is those
few days marked the beginning of my real life.

Anyone who encounters a breakup knows what I mean.
Jesus said, ". . . whosoever will lose his life for my sake
shall find it" (Matthew 16:25).

During those months following that ultimate personal
submission, you begin to understand very clearly that you
indeed lost one life, but began a new, clean, glorious life in
Christ—not self-centered, but Christ-centered! Many times
in years past I had encountered that beautiful Bible passage,
Galatians 2:20, which says:

> I am crucified with Christ: nevertheless I live; yet not I,
> but Christ liveth in me: and the life which I now live in
> the flesh I live by the faith of the Son of God, who loved
> me, and gave himself for me.

I knew that verse, I thought, but I had not experienced it.
I had not been to Calvary. Why does it take us so long?
Why are we so afraid to die? What are we afraid we'll lose?
Only our selves—those cumbersome, troublesome selves we
really don't know what to do with.

It was like the time we gave the twins up to God. They
were premature, very tiny, and the doctors told Bob and me
that Billy and Barbara were dying. Brother Bill Chapman,
our beloved pastor, visited us at my hospital bed and told
us, as we wept bitterly, that we must give God free access to
our babies.

I felt so afraid to do that because I was convinced He

surely would take them. For Bob especially, that was an ag-
onizing prayer to pray. But in the end, what else could we
do? And then He *really* gave them to us—gave them in such
a miraculous way!

Often when I give my testimony publicly, I tell about the
twins. And though they are seven and one-half now, two
bright and beautiful miracles, the story is as fresh and marvelous to Bob and me as when it first happened. I still cry
when I tell it.

Looking back, I see the Lord has faithfully trained us in
submitting to one another from the very beginning. It seems
ages ago, during those first rocky, stormy years of marriage,
when Bob and I would get on our knees and beg God to
save it.

Then came our crisis with the twins, and again we had no
choice but to submit to God's will for us and for our family.

A series of deaths—precious family members and irre-
placeable friends—brought Bob and me to the point of ques-
tioning God, holding out against His will for a time, and
then to our own surrender.

Eventually, profoundly, I came to my own Calvary experience. This is the submission that teaches the *joy* of submission. This is the death that produces free, joyous, healthy
life!

It teaches a woman what a privilege she has as a wife
when she yields herself to her husband. And I'm learning
that this goes, not only for Bob, but also for the children. I
asked God to allow me to not only discipline and disciple
them but to serve them as He would have them served,
remembering the words of Jesus:

And whosoever will be chief among you, let him be
your servant:

Even as the Son of man came not to be ministered unto,
but to minister

Matthew 20:27-28

I've really sought the Lord for ways to minister to Bob
and the children, beginning first with the willingness to let
Him deal with me in my heart and in my spirit.

At one time I took Marabel Morgan's Total Woman
course and used all the techniques she advocates—dressing
up and candlelight dinners, the whole bit—but *without* allowing the Lord to shape my attitude. Mere techniques
without the right spirit simply amount to manipulation—
which the Lord and Marabel never advocated!

So nowadays it all begins with submitting first unto the
Lord, even as David did when he prayed:

Create in me a clean heart, O God; and renew a right
spirit within me.

Cast me not away from thy presence; and take not thy
holy spirit from me.

Psalms 51:10-11

It's always the little things—the little *daily* things—that
test us the most. After all, when we're confronted with the
major moral choices, the big, life-changing decisions,
they're usually pretty clear-cut.

But the little matters color the whole of life. For example, I believe love and sex begin early in the day. The

lovemaking at night really grows out of the whole day's caring which includes taking that minute to pour fresh, chilled Florida orange juice, to remember the vitamin tablets, to brew fresh coffee, to add a flower, and to take them upstairs with a happy attitude and a moment of cheerful conversation.

To make personal contact, real contact, with that man first thing in the day, before the rest of the world crowds in on him—that, friends, is submission to God's priorities. After all, only one woman in all the world is appointed by God to minister to Bob in these small ways.

As the years go by, it's easy to allow relationships to become impersonal. It just naturally happens, and if there are problems arising too, well, there's no desire to do the little things for one another. Or if you're uptight, snowed under, and becoming a real victim of self-pity, you sure don't want to go out of your way to do something for him. This can get to be habitual.

In that case, ask God to deal with your attitudes. Submit —first to God—then to the man you love. You'll never regret it!

Sadly enough, for years Bob put out fresh flowers for me —beautiful roses usually, in the breakfast room or on my desk or bedside table—and did other similar little personal things for me. However, I stayed so self-absorbed, so busy, that these touches usually went unacknowledged. Now I catch these things, and they mean a lot to me.

How many roses do we overlook, how many chances to say I love you? And how many days, girls, do we waste by remaining totally preoccupied with self?

The good news is God gladly sets these things in order

within our lives the moment we're ready for Him to do so. It just takes getting down on our knees and getting right with the Lord.

Each day we must start with a submissive attitude toward God, stay confessed and prayed up, praise the Lord in all things and remember:

> Trust in the Lord with all thine heart; and lean not unto thine own understanding;
> In all thy ways acknowledge him, and he shall direct thy paths.

Proverbs 3:5–6

Then will God send us His great gifts of love, joy, and peace.

Oh, yes, there are still those mornings when I blow it, especially when I've worked late the night before. I may be totally wretched, but I know why, and I know to go to my Source and get right. And He forgives me as I submit and start over again—and the love and joy and peace return!

Praise the Lord!

6

Farfar's Salvation

As I CHOSE a title for this chapter, I realized how many years Bob and I longed to write those words.

How long? Forever, it seems.

And why? Because Farfar—whose real name was Einar Green—was Bob's father. He was a tall, strong Swedish-born man, a gentle person who adored his grandchildren. But he also was very stubborn about one thing; he did not want to hear anything about Jesus Christ and his own need for salvation.

Einar and Svea Green, Bob's parents, immigrated from Sweden to New York City where they struggled hard to make a living. Bob, their only child, knew plenty about hard times, but he also knew about character, decency, hard work, and how to have fun even when your family didn't have much money.

Eventually the Greens moved to Florida, where Bob became a well-known broadcasting personality and everyone flourished. After Bob and I married and the babies arrived, Einar and Svea Green became Farfar and Farmor (*father's father* and *father's mother* in Swedish). They became extremely important to our kids, and especially to Bobby and

Gloria. Farfar and Farmor always came in and kept the children when Bob and I had bookings, and their help is what made the whole thing possible. We could not have left our children with just anyone!

As the years rolled forward, one by one the members of our household committed their lives to Jesus Christ. And as we grew in our knowledge of the Lord, and as He became central to our lives, more and more each one of us yearned to see Farfar and Farmor accept Jesus.

If you have read any of our earlier books, you know how we witnessed to them. You know the many times Bob claimed the Scripture Acts 16:31 which says, "Believe on the Lord Jesus Christ, and thou shalt be saved, and thy house." Bob and I claimed that Scripture entirely by faith in the Word of God, for over the years despite testimonies, prayers, and faithful intercession by many, many members of the Body of Christ, Farfar and Farmor refused to relent. They would not or could not believe, and they refused to fake it.

"The hardest people to lead to the Lord," Bob once said, "are good people. They know they are not wicked, and they see no need for any change in their lives."

> He that believeth on him is not condemned: but he that believeth not is condemned already, because he hath not believed in the name of the only begotten Son of God.
>
> John 3:18

"The second hardest people are members of your own family. They know too much about you; they're skeptical!

A rare moment when the active Green family is still.

The addition to Villa Verde is finally begun, proving you can't outgive God. *Below:* Ready to challenge the slopes at Sun Valley.

Barbara's lines steal the show, while Gloria delivers some fine acting in *Sound of Music. Below:* Bobby, Billy, and Bob are no strangers to the kitchen or the importance of nutrition.

Barbara Peterson—Miss U.S.A., Lenne Jo Hallgren—America's Junior Miss, Katherine Durden—Miss Teenage America, and Deana Jo Harragarra—Miss American Indian join Bob and me backstage of the July 4 special, "Stars and Stripes Show". *Below:* Taking time out from rehearsal for a Sunday-school lesson with the Coogans, a drill team of committed Christians from Ada, Oklahoma.

Stirring things up while cohosting the Mike Douglas Show from
Disney World. *Below:* That week we became friends with Dean Jones,
the Disney actor who is a great Christian brother.

Gloria cuddles Muffin, a gift from Charlie and Marabel Morgan. *Below:* Bobby, who thrives on athletics, keeps his bike in shape too. That's Bob's '56 T-bird with the DEACON plates behind Bobby.

The parakeets, Perky and Frostie, get a nibble from Barbara. *Below:* Billy's pet, Waldo the Basset Hound, bites the toe (hand) that feeds him.

Sharing Farfar's first Easter after his salvation. *Below:* Farfar is presented with a Swedish Bible upon becoming a master of Bredablick Masonic Lodge.

We've got to pray hard, because we have both those strikes against us," Bob said.

Meanwhile, Farfar's health began to slip. During the past three years he encountered major surgery more than once, besides enduring a fall that broke two ribs, suffering small strokes, and undergoing such age-related difficulties as hardening of the arteries. His normally sweet nature gave way to bad temper at times, and he grew increasingly hard to handle.

Bob and I and the children, with numerous friends and all the saints at Northwest Baptist Church where we worship, made Farfar the object of continuing prayer. Each of our children literally has prayed for their grandparents' salvation all their lives. And in the end, God used our daughter, Gloria Lynn, as an instrument in Farfar's salvation.

March 4, 1976. We'll remember that date forever. That morning at the invitation of our friend, Al Chubb, we did the Greater Orlando Mayor's Prayer Breakfast, which hosted a number of visiting mayors and other public officials. Everybody was interested in politics just then; so I said to them, "I'm here to announce my candidacy today, as a representative of Jesus Christ." Everyone laughed.

Later that day we traveled to Plant City for the Strawberry Festival, and there I did two more shows. That's one of our favorite festivals, and we had a ball. We have been there before at the invitation of Louise Gibbs. As manager of the Strawberry Festival, she provides strong Christian leadership which makes a performance there very rewarding. But by the time we packed and flew back to Miami Beach, arriving about two in the morning, we were exhausted. Despite my fatigue, I always bring back strawber-

ries to make preserves which I call Praise the Lord Anyway
Strawberry Preserves.

When I woke up the next morning, I felt so tired, my
body ached all over. To make matters worse, each one of
the kids was strung out and having problems and everything
needed doing at once. It was the kind of morning when you
just think *What's the use?* And somewhere in the midst of
all that, the thought popped into my head, "I think I'll
never write another book unless Farfar gets saved." Don't
ask me what that had to do with anything, but that's what I
thought.

Lo and behold, Bob phoned me that afternoon and asked,
"What were we doing yesterday afternoon at 4:30?" I
wasn't in the mood. I was sitting at my desk, really having a
pity party, still tired and out-of-sorts.

"I don't know," I grumped. "You were there. You know
what was going on as well as I do."

"Well, yesterday afternoon at 4:30," Bob said, "Farfar
got saved."

"Farfar got—*what?*" By now I was sitting up, wide
awake, wanting to believe it but not ready to.

"You've got to be kidding," I said. "Are you sure?"

And then he told me the story, and I just broke down and
bawled. Then Bob started crying and neither one of us
could talk. We just held the phone and wept.

"While we were gone—," Bob choked. "Nobody we
knew—."

"Come on home," was all I could say.

It didn't seem possible. For the past year or more, we had
been through such decision-making times with Bob's parents. We had experienced so many things with them, espe-

cially with Farfar, but the power of God was so present in our home, and we prayed so much about what to do next, that God always saw us through.

We asked God to show us how to love our parents and encourage them, yet not baby or pamper them. It was hard to know how to cope with the changes in Farfar sometimes, especially the sudden rages, when he'd roar at the children and get all upset.

It wasn't easy for him or for anybody else, but we felt our children needed to understand that their grandfather needed extra love from all of us. We wanted to demonstrate love and loyalty and family solidarity as things grew tough for Farmor and Farfar.

When it seemed that stubbornness and noncooperation would show up, we'd give it to the Lord. We'd ask Him for extra patience and understanding and enough love.

The arteriosclerosis created personality changes in Farfar, and he'd sometimes act very childish and hard to handle. Eventually vascular surgery was recommended, and it had to be done in Miami Beach. While he was in the hospital, Farmor stayed with us. Despite the worry and tension in the situation, God's grace abounded. Bob and I had a terrible, hectic schedule at that time too, but God provided.

During those days Brother Claude Wilson from our church witnessed to Farfar, but he still wouldn't accept Christ. Brother Wilson just continued to visit and fellowship and kept the door open—and waited on the Lord. Farfar began to love Brother Wilson and look forward to his visits.

Gloria Roe Robertson, Jody Dunton, and so many other friends ministered and witnessed to him, and loved him. Meanwhile, Farmor faithfully visited his hospital room almost every day. At last, she was so worn out that I insisted she go home for a weekend and let me sit with Farfar each afternoon as much as possible. She reluctantly agreed to let us take her home and went along with Gloria Roe Robertson and me as we traveled to Bibletown for a concert.

As we drove, God let me talk to Gloria in Farmor's presence in ways I never could have done otherwise, and at the concert she heard me give much of my testimony. I was able that night to be really gut-level honest in my testimony, and I knew God gave me the words that spoke to her directly.

I could admit I had not always been the Christian daughter-in-law God wanted me to be—and there were other things I could say that I knew spoke to her. Afterwards she told me, "That was really wonderful."

But it's not words, after all, but how you live your life. Farmor has observed these past two years more love, patience, and self-control in our household—those things the Bible calls gifts of the Holy Spirit—and she knows we give God the credit. She won't admit it, but she knows these do not come from us!

The following Monday Bob had to work in the office; so Pedro, who is our chauffeur, handyman, and right arm at Villa Verde, and I checked Farfar out of the hospital in Miami Beach and took him home, only to discover he had tried to get out of bed and had suffered a little fall. They put a harness on him to keep him securely in bed.

Once at his home in Boynton Beach, we realized Farmor couldn't handle him unless we strapped him to the bed, and he insisted on getting up and doing his own thing. We knew he might fall again. And because the nurse we had hired had not yet arrived, we didn't dare leave Farmor there to try to cope alone. Meanwhile, he wanted to be untied, but I said no.

At that, Farfar burst into a torrent of Swedish and got really mad at me. At last he said in English, "You don't love me." That's the only time he ever said such a thing.

"Farfar," I told him, "the trouble is I *do* love you. Now you lie down this minute and behave yourself or we'll have to send you back to the hospital." He obeyed.

I was really firm with him. "Don't you tell me I don't love you; I love you with all my heart," I said. "But you're going to have to cooperate until the nurse arrives tomorrow."

The next day, even before the nurse arrived, it became obvious that Farmor couldn't cope. She had to put him into the hospital in Boynton Beach even before we knew about it. Farmor was under such a terrible strain. We were out of town when the bad news came, and I felt so terrible about it that I wanted to go get him and take care of him myself; yet I couldn't. There was no way. The schedule was unbelievable.

So I went into a big, big depression about Farfar. And the whole time, God was working things out.

We were upset that Farmor had put him into the hospital and later—so unwillingly—we had to put him in the adjacent convalescent home; yet the hospital is where God chose for Farfar to accept Jesus.

Farfar's nurses were Christians. None witnessed to him, but they all gave him the love and tenderness he so desperately needed.

Frequently Brother Wilson visited Farfar in the hospital

in Miami Beach and witnessed to him a little. On one occasion, he said, "Farfar, wouldn't you like to take this opportunity to invite Jesus into your heart?"

"No."

"But will you someday?" Brother Wilson asked.

"Yes," Farfar said.

That was the first time Farfar ever said yes to a salvation question, so we felt encouraged.

But that day at the Plant City Strawberry Festival, only a few days after Farmor had returned Farfar to the hospital, the last thing Bob and I were thinking of was Farfar's salvation. After having just been released from one hospital, we were upset that Farfar had been placed in another hospital. But God was on the ball.

The story is simplicity itself—a lonely, frustrated old man, ill and impatient, and a sympathetic nurse, attempting to minister to his physical needs. "Let's walk down the corridor, Sweetheart," she soothed him, and Farfar obediently allowed her to lead him in a walk. She talked to him and tried to cheer him, and when they returned to his room, she noticed one of my books beside his bed.

"I knew who he was, and I knew about you," Jo Sargeant later told me. "I assumed he surely must be a born-again Christian." Jo and her husband, who are missionaries, had begun, independent of any established missionary board, Camp Maranatha in Del Ray Beach, Florida, for kids to come to know Christ.

Seated in his wheelchair, Farfar listened as Jo read some cards and messages to him. "A lady from Oklahoma had written about how God healed her, and when I read her note, he started crying," she said. "After reading several others, we came to a card from Gloria Lynn, which said: 'Farfar, we're praying for you to be healed, but more importantly, we're praying for you to ask Jesus into your heart.'"

That was Jo Sargeant's first indication that Farfar was unsaved. "People have prayed for you for many years haven't they?" she asked gently. He began to cry again and nodded his head.

The Lord began to speak to Farfar in the simplest of terms through his nurse. She told him the good news and led him through the plan of salvation, and then she said, "Farfar, wouldn't you like to ask God into your heart?"

"Yes."

They knelt down, he bowed his head, and she led him in the prayer of commitment. Now Farfar had a speech problem resulting from his physical condition. Often he couldn't coordinate his thoughts and his speech, and he'd end up stuttering and furious. But Jo said when he prayed the sinner's prayer, every word came out clear as a bell.

Afterwards, realizing his mental and emotional condition, Jo Sargeant questioned him: "Farfar, do you know what you have done?" She wanted to be sure he knew—and he did.

Once J. Harold Smith, the famous evangelist, came to lunch at our house while Farfar was there. I had them sit in the courtyard and chat while I prepared lunch, and everything in the kitchen went wrong. The microwave oven wouldn't work, the bread didn't arrive, and the fire in the grill went out three times under the steaks. Brother Smith said later, "I was praying the whole time that something would detain you while we talked."

His prayers and mine were answered. That was the worst experience with lunch I'd ever had in my life!

Brother Smith prayed for Farfar that day, and among other things, asked God to make him miserable until he came to his salvation. Later, when I reminded Farfar of that prayer, he snapped, "I really don't think that was very nice!" But he knew he was just holding out on God, for whatever reason.

Who knows? Don't we all hold out on Him—totally or partially? Haven't we all done what Farfar was doing? Because if we keep back even a tiny corner of our lives, we're holding out.

The following day, Jo Sargeant chose a good time for Farfar, then rang our house as we had requested and put him on the phone. The first thing he told us was, "I got saved."

"Praise God. We're so happy, and we love you so much," we said, and we all cried. We let all the kids take turns speaking to their grandfather, and they told him they were proud of him and loved him very much.

From then on we prayed with him, and we saw such a difference in his spirit. He still couldn't talk well, but the fits of temper mostly subsided, and he smiled a lot and regained so much of his sweetness.

Jo Sargeant said not only did Farfar understand what he had done, but several times he asked her to pray with him. She said instead of being difficult, he became just like a lamb.

After Farfar was saved, he lay back on his bed and said, "Jesus loves me. Jesus loves me. Jesus loves me." And then somehow Jo Sargeant knew to lean forward and sing that little song to him.

"I'm certainly no singer, Miss Bryant," she told me, "but somehow I knew he had heard 'Jesus Loves Me' at some point in his life."

Farfar, who was an orphan, had felt rejection several times in foster homes and had never experienced any kind of parental love.

"Oh, God," I said, "what a ministering angel you sent to Farfar to lead him like a little child right into the Kingdom of Heaven!"

One day I took Mother over to the convalescent home to see Farfar, because she hadn't seen him in a long time. Somehow I ended up in the lobby, singing "How Great Thou Art" and giving my testimony to the old folks, and Farfar cried the whole time.

Another time, after Farfar had been transferred to Villa Maria, a convalescent home in Miami, so we could be nearer to him, we came in from a heavy schedule, so fatigued and tired, we were tempted not to attend Sunday school and church. Something told me I must go. So we went, and I taught Sunday school, and before going to lunch, we all went to see Farfar and wheeled him outside in the sunshine for a little visit.

I felt led to share with him some of my girls' Sunday school lesson and to read a few scriptures. Then we all joined hands as a family, but before Bob led us in prayer, the Lord led me to suggest to Farfar that he tell our children about his conversion—and yet, I knew he couldn't talk well enough to tell the story.

"The children know about your conversion from us," I

explained. "But Farfar, if you want them to know that you understood what you did, and that you are glad you are saved, could you just say, *Thank You, Jesus?*"

Without hesitating, he said, "Thank You, Jesus," in his Swedish accent, and he was crying. The children's mouths flew open in surprise. They looked so touched and impressed.

"That's your first public witness, Farfar," I told him. So we held hands, and Bob prayed and thanked God that we are a family, not just related by human blood lines, but also adopted into the family of God by faith. We knew our children never would forget that moment. How important it was that we obeyed God that day!

We've described this salvation story at length for more reasons than one. The story actually belongs to the hundreds of people we know about, who through the years, were faithful to pray and witness in person. We have no idea how many of our readers God also touched in behalf of Bob's father and mother.

The entire process took at least sixteen years that our family knows of. So many people prayed for him, including our whole church, and so many had witnessed to him, but in the final analysis, it was as easy as rolling off a log.

Peggy Chapman, our pastor's wife, said it best: "Isn't it just like God to bring us all back to the point of simplicity?"

How good that Gloria was blessed to be God's instrument in her grandfather's salvation. She loved him so much, as did all the kids.

"What if you had not written that note?" I asked her. "What if you had been afraid of his rejection?" It was so good for her, and for all of us, to understand the importance of being obedient to the guidance of God's Holy Spirit and holding fast to the faith.

How much our Lord yearns over one lost soul: and how faithful He is to those who place their trust in Him. For you see, exactly five months from the day Farfar came to Christ, he went home to live with Him forever.

Praise God!

7

Confessions of a Foodaholic

AFTER READING OUR previous books in which I talked about diet and exercise, people write and say, "I wish I could be like you."

Well don't. I am a foodaholic. I admit it; so why do I take that first cooky? The devil loves meeting up with a guy like me. He knows the chink in my armor okay, and usually tries to stuff it with something sweet, gooey, and chocolate!

In fighting the battle of the bulge, I confess I still don't have it made. Through diet, determination, and discipline you can take that weight off all right, but you don't dare relax your guard for a moment.

A foodaholic had better recognize himself for what he is, or he will trip up on something stupid every time—like eating three bags of popcorn at the movies or discovering that one last piece of pie when you're looking in the fridge for skim milk! Would you believe my latest dietary transgressions actually occurred as I was getting together my notes for this chapter!

It all started very innocently when I met former Oakland A's manager, Alvin Dark, for a business lunch to discuss his bookings through Fishers of Men and he remarked that I was in pretty good shape. It's nice to get that kind of compliment from an athlete, so I felt good.

"Yeah, Al, I'm watching my diet," I said.

"Where do you want to eat lunch?"

"I don't know. I don't eat lunch," I told him. So we went to this real nice French restaurant, and we ate and ate and ate. (It's a shame to let fine food like that go to waste, isn't it?)

When you blow it that thoroughly, it usually goes from bad to worse—in this case, it went into my helping with Gloria's birthday party. *Helping* (or *helpings*) is the right word too—helpings of candy, pizza, cake, and ice cream, you name it. My orgy lasted for three days as I impulsively stuffed my face with all kinds of forbidden fruit.

We don't laugh anymore when I act like that. The kids realize Daddy-the-cooky-sneak doesn't live here anymore, and they're the first to try to help me fight the good fight.

The good life is killing Americans these days. Doctors say three quarters of all deaths in America each year stem from diseases related to affluence—from smoking, obesity, and lack of exercise. "Where else in our world do people smoke themselves to death, drink themselves to death, and even eat themselves to death?" one doctor challenged.

It's shocking to realize that medical science can battle infectious diseases almost to a standstill—but doctors can't figure out how to stop us from smoking, eating, and lazing ourselves to death!

Interestingly enough, the Bible tells us in Deuteronomy 21:18–23 that if a man has a stubborn and rebellious son who refuses to obey and is a drunkard and a glutton, his parents should bring him to the gates of the city, and he should be stoned to death.

Now that's strong stuff! It gives some indication that God doesn't take the sin of gluttony lightly. In fact, one of the strong accusations hurled against Jesus was that He was "a winebibber and a glutton" (*see* Matthew 11:19, Luke 7:34), and you know they were constantly seeking reasons to put Him to death.

Presently some 70 million Americans suffer from obesity. "Some people drink themselves into an early grave, others achieve the same result with a lavish intake of potatoes and cream gravy," a country newspaper reported.

It's true. If you are one of America's 70 million foodaholics, as I am, or if some member of your family commits the sin of gluttony, it's time to begin to call it what it is. You can help yourself or that family member by facing facts right now, speaking the truth in love, and asking God to help overcome this problem.

God told the apostle Paul, "My grace is sufficient for thee: for my strength is made perfect in weakness" (2 Corinthians 12:9). It's important to remember He does provide the strength, when we admit our weakness. It has been my experience that our own willpower does not go far enough over the long haul.

But even though you're not overweight, you still can cheat yourself drastically—and the Lord, too—every time you sit down at the table. Cheating nutritionally, that is.

Quinn Buckner, the six-foot-three-inch Indiana strongman who was team captain and All-Big-Ten guard, slipped into near obscurity last year, possibly because of "a costly dalliance with junk food," an AP news story reported.

Buckner, who gave up a starting job for the Indiana foot-
ball team, had been the Hoosiers' undisputed floor leader in
basketball for four years. He earned first-team All-Con-
ference and honorable mention All-America honors, but
midway in the season he went into a terrible slump and was
benched for the first time in his career.

"His stamina was poor, his shooting was even worse, he
made silly errors, and committed unnecessary fouls," the
story continued. After being totally overlooked when it
came time to pass out honors, player Buckner and his coach
doggedly sought to discover the reason for the dramatic
nose dive.

"I wasn't eating the right foods," the twenty-two-year-old
senior finally concluded. Buckner, as many seniors do,
moved into his own apartment last year. "I was eating ham-
burgers and french fries and not getting the vegetables and
vitamins you need," he said.

Later the athlete discovered that when his diet improved,
so did his game.

Poor nutrition not only accounts for dramatic loss of
physical and mental efficiency, but doctors say it also may
help cause one-half of the cancers in women and one-third
of those in men.

"Evidence is now at hand that nutrition—not so much in
terms of food additives or food contaminants, but rather
specific deficiencies and excesses—significantly contributes
to the development of a whole variety of human cancers,"
said Dr. Ernst L. Wynder of the American Health Federa-
tion.

Two of the biggest killers in the nation, cancer of the
colon and the breast, have been associated with *malnu-*

trition of the affluent. In the case of colon cancer, a diet low in fiber and high in fat is blamed. And breast cancer has been linked to a high-fat diet.

Fiber speeds up elimination of the contents of the intestinal tract, doctors explain, which cuts the absorption of dangerous fats and cholesterol into the blood. It speeds away from the intestines, the bacteria that produce chemicals and increase the risk of colon cancer.

In countries where fiber is a standard part of the diet, there are fewer cases of some types of cancer, diabetes, heart disease, and obesity.

And then, of course, there are those who are overweight. Doctors agree that in general, Americans are too fat. "There is no known increased risk of any disease until a person weighs 30 percent over the standards set by insurance companies—a very noticeable weight gain," said Dr. Margaret MacKenzie. "Once the level is exceeded, then the risk of all diseases increases, including the risk of cancer and of accidents, not merely heart disease," she wrote in a recent issue of *Obesity—Bariatric Medicine.*

That gives us some idea of how much most of us need to learn, and be willing to change. The fact is, *it's a sin the way most Americans eat!*

We're not attempting to give dietary advice, of course, but Anita and I pray that more Christians will begin to seek the Lord about these things. God's word warns us not to abuse the temple of the Holy Spirit. It's interesting that those people who continue to live according to strict biblical precepts—notably the Mormons and the Seventh-Day Adventists—suffer only half as many cancer and heart attack deaths as the rest of the population.

The Adventists also record a 68 percent lower rate of deaths from respiratory disease, a 46 percent lower death rate from strokes, and a 93 percent lower death rate from cirrhosis of the liver.

Dr. John Farquhar, director of the Heart Disease Prevention Program at Stanford University, said there's a lesson to be learned from those figures. He says people who have a high risk of disease because of obesity, high blood pressure, and high cholesterol levels, should change their dietary habits.

He recommends you simply modify your diet a little to make significant changes for the better. For example:

1. Throw away the saltshaker to cut your salt intake in half.
2. Get down to your ideal weight and do not add pounds after age twenty.
3. Eliminate saturated fats (fats that solidify at room temperature).
4. Eat more fruits, vegetables, and other foods containing fiber (generally the nondigestible parts of food in vegetables such as carrots and potatoes; legumes such as beans, peas, and lentils; fruits, and grain).

In battling excess weight, I found I needed to work like a detective to figure out when I ate what and for what reasons. Overeating often comes from emotional needs or from dumb habit. It's important to figure yourself out when you're trying to outwit those old, ingrained sinful habits.

Food serves a lot of nonfood purposes, psychiatrists say, and we who are overweight rarely eat a lot because we are hungry. People are conditioned to eat at a certain time, such as eating during the TV news or joining the kids when they have an afternoon snack.

The desire to eat also arises from such things as loneliness, boredom, frustration, or anger; so it's my job to figure out what's really happening when I go berserk and start stuffing my face.

Okay, so how do we turn ourselves around?

We can seek the Lord to discover the reasons—which can be hidden down there pretty deep—for habitual overeating. We can ask Him to make us willing to be willing to try to change our lives.

The next step is to get dietary advice from your doctor and follow it. Learn what you are doing and why.

One of the most important things to remember is eat at the proper time—and enjoy your food. Pause between bites. Delay between courses. Slow down and enjoy the conversation. Ask for seconds if you want them, but never allow anyone to serve you seconds unless you ask.

One thing that helps me is that I make a conscious effort to enjoy my family. We always try to be together at mealtimes, and we have some pretty lively conversation. Mealtimes are entertaining at our house. There's no desire to put your face down in your plate and silently shove the food in when you have funny conversation going on. We really make an effort to have things pleasant, and this encourages each of us to eat properly.

Dr. Lester Breslow, dean of the School of Public Health at the University of California at Los Angeles, said that by switching from a bad life-style to a more healthful one, a person can add about fourteen years to his life.

A five and one-half year study of seven thousand scientifically selected adults who live in northern California revealed that certain health habits are associated with a longer life, Dr. Breslow said. He gave seven of those habits which make up a healthy life-style:

1. Eat three meals at regular times each day instead of snacking.
2. Eat breakfast every day.
3. Get moderate exercise (long walks, bike riding, swimming, gardening).
4. Sleep seven or eight hours a night.
5. Do not smoke.
6. Maintain moderate weight.
7. Do not consume alcohol to an immoderate degree.

(He defines moderate consumption as three ounces of alcohol daily. Of course I strongly believe that even one ounce of alcohol is one ounce too many.)

Dr. Breslow's study showed that a forty-five-year-old man who practiced three or less of these healthier habits may expect to live to age sixty-seven. A man with six or seven of these habits can expect to live to be eighty-one.

How does that list check out at your house? Why not have every family member take a look, and if everyone would change even just one bad health habit, imagine the improvements in your household! I believe God expects us men, as heads of our households, to set this type of example.

Someone sent me a fantastic little article called "Dieting with Jesus" written by a housewife who said she has lost several hundred pounds—by first gaining weight, then losing it, over and over. Sound familiar?

Melba Ward, in *Aglow* magazine, tells how to maintain an ideal weight:

1.   Admit you are overweight; "The truth shall make you free" (John 8:32).
2.   Know you cannot control your weight by your own strength. You never have been able to and you never will (*see* Romans 7:18).
3.   Know that "with God all things are possible" (Matthew 19:26).
4.   Determine in your heart that whatever it takes, you will "deny yourself, take up your cross, and follow Jesus" (*see* Matthew 16:24).
5.   Recognize how deliverance from overweight works: you sow seeds (cut calories) and Jesus delivers you of pounds. The harvest is the Lord's.
6.   Sow your seeds in joy (*see* 2 Corinthians 9:7).
7.   If loss of pounds comes to a halt, check to see if you are:

   a.   cutting enough calories
   b.   dieting in joy
   c.   giving God the glory (and not self)
   d.   resting in His love and grace

8.   BE HONEST. When Satan attacks, admit your weakness, declare God's power in you, quote Scripture (*see* 1 John 4:4), and command him to leave in Jesus' name by the power of the Blood (*see* James 4:7).
9.   When circumstances cause you to go off the diet for one meal, tell the Lord in advance what's happening—don't

just break your promise. The Lord hates lying (Proverbs 6:16–17).

It's a battle, and with me it takes place daily. I know it always will be that way, because foodaholics can't relax their vigilance.

Dr. William Saunders, an Austell, Georgia physician, referred to that promise when he said, "We can live seventy years now. I don't know how long we could live if we practiced good health—at least 150 years.

"In the Bible people lived 800 or 900 years. I thought they used different measures of time, but I wonder now."

In the Book of Proverbs, God continually exhorts us toward wise and prudent living. He gives us many rules for moderation, including one we dieters could well adopt:

> My son, forget not my law; but let thine heart keep my commandments;
> For length of days, and long life, and peace, shall they add to thee.
>
> Proverbs 3:1–2

Amen!

8

Confessions of a Spendaholic

MANY CHRISTIANS believe God did our country a favor by allowing the recent economic recession to occur.

Are we Americans spoiled? Have we become greedy and materialistic, as our critics say? Do we take our affluence for granted? Do we love money too much?

There are as many answers to those questions, I feel certain, as there are households. All I know is the Bob Green household has raised these questions a lot recently. We have become aware of money and stewardship, and God's purposes versus ours.

God has dealt with me, in particular, about money. I am a spendaholic, and God has had to show me this. The subject of money pains me and embarrasses me, and all my life I've run away from facing reality in this area.

But when we bring ourselves totally to the Lord, He is faithful to point out our sins and weaknesses. He's helping me change my spending habits—which I admit have been atrocious. He's also casting the light of His truth on exactly how childish and irresponsible I have been in the past where money was concerned.

The more it hurts, the more I have to admit I'm learning

some necessary lessons. Going on periodic spending sprees is something I've never been proud to admit.

Instead of discussing the problem with your husband in a mature way afterward, a spending spree often leads to having a little temper fit or refusing to discuss the subject at all —which doesn't solve anything. It means dreading to see bills come in, dreading to discuss them, and then, if you can't avoid the subject, taking the attitude, "As hard as I work, how dare you say I can't buy that?" And all the time you *are* working hard, sure, but you're also working hard at spending. And then refusing to look at the totals.

Well girls, the Lord can reach us spendaholics even when our husbands can't. And when God begins to convict you of your own immaturity—well, it breaks your heart.

A number of years back, when Bob and I had a showdown about tithing, my education began. Phil Braunstein, our accountant, was working with Bob that day. My only contribution to the session was to inform them—once more— that God expects us to tithe.

"But Anita, do you know how many *dollars* that would be?" Bob asked me. Then he and Phil had to show me—in black and white—the amazing columns of figures I had always refused to look at. When I looked at the actual totals of the dollars I was spending, then looked at our tremendous overhead, for the first time, I realized Bob really *was* helpless where the tithe was concerned. Unless I would work with him, we could not obey God.

Bring ye all the tithes into the storehouse, that there may be meat in mine house, and prove me now herewith, saith the LORD of hosts, if I will not open you the windows

of heaven, and pour you out a blessing, that there shall not
be room enough to receive it.

I knew that Scripture, Malachi 3:10, and I yearned to
obey it. That day Bob and I, with Phil's approval, decided
to put God first in our finances.

"Only one other client of mine does this," Phil told us.
"But from the time he started, God proceeded to bless him.
You can't outgive God!"

All that happened a number of years ago, and we did
learn you can't outgive God. Again and again His words
proved true.

Honour the LORD with thy substance, and with the
firstfruits of all thine increase:
So shall thy barns be filled with plenty, and thy presses
shall burst out with new wine.

Proverbs 3:9–10

As we worked hard, and God increased us, we did experience the joy of giving for the upbuilding of His Kingdom
and the contentment of remaining faithful to Him. None
of that, however, really reached or revealed a central fact
about me which God knew and I still refused to admit; *I am
a spendaholic.*

Then came the economic crunch. It did not affect us
dollarwise, particularly; certainly our family did not lack.
The timing, however, happened to coincide with my realiza-
tion that when I spent money without reason—as I did from
time to time, simply buying anything I saw that I wanted,

never stopping to ask myself if it were needed or even really desired—I was in sin.

The Lord had begun to convict me about this. Not only did I recognize my sinfulness, I feared my own cravings and really hated my weakness in this behavior.

The only thing you can do, of course, is go to the Lord and work things out on your knees. He had to start me at ground zero to begin the financial education I had always refused to consider.

He's having to restrain me every time I go out to shop. I literally pray before I step into a store.

Worse still, He has brought me face to face with the root cause of my extravagance, which is a deep-seated fear of becoming poor again. That's so hard to admit! It's so hard to examine your values in the light of what the Lord expects —and to see that they don't measure up. And it hurts to confront yourself with the fact that you don't trust the Lord perfectly, whether it's reflected in a fear of poverty, or however else it might appear.

The Bible tells us that "Perfect love casteth out fear: because fear hath torment" (1 John 4:18). I could only confess these unworthy fears to God and ask Him to help me.

Little by little He has helped me change my spending habits. It was hard in the past to see something I wanted and not allow myself to have it. Now I weigh the facts, ask myself if it's really worth the money, and force myself to learn what things should cost.

Jesus said, "For unto whomsoever much is given, of him shall be much required" (Luke 12:48). Bob feels accountable to God for his business, family, church responsibilities, and now our stewardship. How can any woman do less than uphold such a Christian husband?

So God convicts me of my carelessness, though I dislike everything about money lessons. I realize I must learn to comparison shop, must know when to buy and when not to, and why. At times I almost get a cold sweat over making the simplest decisions about spending money. Recently, while trying to decide among several designs and prices of wallpaper, I actually broke down and cried!

Why dwell on all this? Because, girls, "The little foxes spoil the vines" (*see* Song of Solomon 2:15). It's this type of weakness, whether it be in our character or simply lack of experience, that Satan can use.

We all know many examples of how money tempts people. Christians are no exception either! The Bible offers some other stories: remember the rich young ruler? Or what happened to Ananias and Sapphira after they cheated God? And worse of all, Judas—who for money, betrayed his Lord!

When a spendaholic goes shopping, Satan loves to slip in ahead of her. I've taken to praying beforehand, "Lord, help me buy exactly what You want me to have—*and not one thing more!*" Pray that and mean it, and God will help you every time. Otherwise, an innocent shopping trip can result in devastating consequences, especially in certain dress shops!

It happened last fall as I looked for two important work dresses for my nationally televised Orange Bowl Parade and Orange Bowl Classic appearance. There's a budget for wardrobe, but I hadn't bothered to learn what the dresses should cost. I had listened to Bob, however, when he counseled me about my spending habits. I was determined to be sensible.

"Lord, Bob says not to spend too much money. Help me find a modestly priced dress that will do," I prayed as I entered the dressing room. The show's producer had asked me to wear a pale blue dress, and the store's fashion consultant had set aside several for me to try.

One was so perfect, with a lovely neckline, full sleeves, and a beautiful color, that I loved it immediately. Then I looked at the price tag, fifty-four dollars. I couldn't believe what I saw. Even the clerk thought there must have been some mistake.

"Wow, is Bob going to be proud of me!" I told myself, terribly pleased. I could hardly wait to show him how well I had done.

Then I headed toward a second even more exclusive shop to find the other dress I needed—something for the Orange Bowl Classic. I discovered it immediately, a designer original. Fantastic! It was a real knockout.

I must say I have good taste; you should have seen *that* price tag. As I turned and twisted and admired the glittering dress from every possible angle, the face in the mirror looked somewhat dubious, just a little subdued. A small voice was whispering that I had better hold off, that it was a lot of money.

A louder voice was saying, "That's *your* dress, dear. You'll never find a more stunning effect." Suddenly I felt bound and determined to have *that dress*.

"Send it out," I said decisively. "But—could you bill me *after* Christmas?"

"Certainly."

I knew I was going to get in trouble, but maybe I could figure something out, or at least delay the inevitable. So I bragged about the bargain dress, but didn't tell Bob about the other one. I wasted no time in phoning to inquire about my wardrobe budget however, only to confirm what I suspected; I'd blown the budget by a nightmarish amount.

What to do? My cagey little mind went into overdrive at that point. I asked my secretary to have them forward my dress money to me immediately without going through my agent, Dick Shack, or Bob. I'd apply that to the cost of the sinful extravagance, then ask the store to bill me just for the remainder. Even that would be bad enough, but I thought Bob would let it pass.

Well, I got caught, of course. You know the Lord wouldn't let me get away with a trick like that. No way. I had to confess to Bob that I not only overspent, but absolutely threw the budget out the window, plus fouled up the bookkeeping with the whole thing.

I thought I would die. I've seldom in my life been so embarrassed, ashamed, and remorseful—and all over a silly dress! What in the world would my husband say to me?

He just laughed. "Let that teach you a lesson," was all he said—no anger, no sermon, no nothing. I felt totally ashamed.

The interesting thing is Bob never liked that dress, even before he knew what it cost. So the Lord showed me that looking right for a certain occasion doesn't have to have a high price tag to do it—and that *nothing* is worth the price I paid in guilt and stress.

Monetary deceits invariably make us miserable, which is

a good thing. If we were to succeed in those unworthy little plots, we'd continue to get deeper and deeper into trouble, more and more frightened, and there's not always a forgiving Bob around to laugh it off and pay the bill.

Take Gladys, for example. When she first joined our household staff it was on a part-time basis. I soon noticed her wonderful spirit, intelligence, and attitude toward work and concluded that Gladys was an answer to my prayers. She's great.

I didn't know a lot about our smiling new helper, but we all appreciated her. We knew her husband was sick and the family received welfare assistance. I also knew that Gladys wanted her checks made out in her maiden name, but I didn't bother to question her about it.

One day Gladys came to me in great fear. Her welfare caseworker would be phoning me for verification of Gladys' part-time status, she said. Even though she helped us full-time by then, she wanted me to inform the caseworker differently.

"Would you lie for me?" she asked. She had been on tranquilizers, and I could see she was a nervous wreck.

"I couldn't do that," I told her.

She began to cry and told me a neighbor had reported her to welfare officials for receiving her payments from the state while she also was being paid for full-time employment. As she explained that they were after her to pay the money back or face the prospect of jail, she sobbed in real fear.

I realized I had been an unwitting accomplice in Gladys' predicament. I should have questioned why she wanted her checks made out in her maiden name, for one thing. Now she wanted me to lie for her, and I had to say no.

I had second thoughts because I did not want to hurt Gladys, and I questioned whether it was right to tell the truth considering her bitter financial position and the possibility that she could go to jail. How could I, in my life of plenty, even consider jeopardizing Gladys' position, in her life of comparable poverty? I sought help from lawyers I knew. My friend, Charlie Morgan, advised me that although I may hurt her now, in the long run I would only hurt her much more and even myself since every lie has to be covered by another. So I knew then what I had to do all along.

"Your problems will mushroom," I told her. "I won't lie for you." At that, Gladys began to cry harder and to rummage in her pocketbook. I asked what she wanted.

"I need a tranquilizer," she sobbed.

"No, Gladys, you don't need a tranquilizer; you need Jesus," I said, taking her by the hand and leading her to the kitchen table. We sat down together, and I explained the plan of salvation, then led her through the sinner's prayer. She asked Jesus to come into her heart.

"Now, Gladys, I want you to do something very hard," I instructed her. "I want you to telephone your welfare worker and explain the whole situation to her. Confess your wrongdoing, and tell her you're going to make it right.

"Don't worry, because you're not alone. You have Jesus with you now."

She looked scared but picked up the phone. "I'm born again," she told me.

"God will take care of this whole mess," I said. "I don't

know what we can work out, but I know *He* will work it out."

Slowly she dialed the number, and a look of real peace came over her face. Only moments earlier she had been so upset with me because I wouldn't lie, so mad at her neighbor, scared she'd go to jail, and afraid she would lose her husband and children.

I got on the phone first, introduced myself to the social worker, and explained that Gladys had something important to tell. "I want Gladys to talk to you first," I said, "then I'll speak to you again."

Gladys explained the whole situation to her welfare worker, crying a great deal as she confessed. Then I took the phone and asked how I might help. I explained how frightened Gladys was that she might go to jail.

"First of all, she won't go to jail," I was told. "Please tell Gladys that we appreciate her decision to be honest, and we plan to be lenient in her case. We want to help in every way we can."

When I repeated the social worker's words, Gladys cried again. She couldn't believe how compassionate the woman had been—and that best of all, they would let her repay the excess money she had received, in weekly installments. She thought they would demand a huge sum she couldn't produce and then she'd be sent to jail.

Her feelings of joy and relief were pitiful. Later that day, after our emotions had subsided, I wondered if our Spanish-speaking Gladys really understood the commitment she had made to the Lord.

My worries were needless. "Mrs. Green, you should bake me a cake," she remarked.

"A cake, Gladys? Is today your birthday?"

"It's my spiritual birthday!" she said with a radiant smile. I felt so happy to see her laughing face.

Today my Cuban-American friend is all straight with the Lord and straightened out with the welfare department. At least once a day she visits our family prayer altar, and very often she and I pray together about family affairs.

She told a friend, "Mrs. Green is my brother; she led me to Christ." Her English may suffer occasional slipups, but her heart is perfect.

Our family has had two big monetary goals this year, each very important to us. First, we decided to give an offering to our church's bus ministry, which would be our special birthday gift to Jesus.

The other goal involved making a large and expensive addition to our house, in order that each child might have his own bedroom. Bob and I wanted all of the family to sleep in the same wing of our big house; so the costly addition was our only solution.

We talked over what both goals would mean to each of us, and as a family, decided what our priorities would be. Also, we had just bought a small house five minutes away for Farfar and Farmor so they could be near us during Farfar's illness. This stretched our responsibility even more.

Then the battle for self-control began as we included the kids when we discussed various ways to save money and began to implement them. The children decided, for example, that they could forgo summer camp and vacation trips.

As Christmas approached, the Lord laid the idea for a certain sizable sum on my heart which I proposed we might give for the bus ministry. When I mentioned the sum to

Bob, I could see it would be a battle for him. Much as he loves the bus ministry, he felt we simply couldn't afford to give that much money.

But God had proposed the sum to me—a very large amount—and the family talked it over early that fall and decided each one would sacrifice. We'd cut way down on Christmas presents and save money any way we knew how.

None of us liked the idea of not buying Christmas presents, but the kids got around that. They decided to have a garage sale and part with many of their toys. It was their idea, they did all the work and were thrilled with the eighty dollar proceeds. They used this money to buy gifts for their teachers and friends.

As we talked about the bus ministry and discussed the new bedrooms, we showed the kids that all this tremendous expense would require cooperation on the part of each family member. Daddy and Mommie would have to accept quite a few bookings to pay for the new wing. That meant extra-responsible behavior from each child and so on.

The kids responded like troupers; Bob and I were the ones who had problems. As Christmas approached, we planned to forgo sending Christmas cards and buying presents for any but immediate family members, but it began to get tough. And when I thought of shopping for the children —and really sticking to our limit of just three presents per child—I felt almost sick. The kids didn't mind at all, but I felt angry, depressed, and furious. I began to see how for me, Christmas partly means a whirlwind round of shopping and buying, and I didn't want to give that up!

As December approached, Bob couldn't seem to assure me that we would give that large offering the Lord was tugging at me about. "It's your decision, Bob," was all I said, and, of course, as head of the family it *is* Bob's place to decide. But you gals know how that feels!

As December wore on and I wondered what Bob would do, it became increasingly hard for me to stay quiet and not intervene, but I had to leave it up to him and the Lord. I bit my tongue and prayed a lot.

At last it was time to give our family's birthday gift to Jesus. When Bob handed me the check it was made out for the amount God had placed on my heart, and I screamed!

Bob looked kind of funny. "We must not give this money unless we can do it with a happy heart," I said immediately. "If we give it grudgingly, it's really not a gift at all."

"Take it," Bob said. I looked at him, but couldn't read his face. "Take it," he repeated. "It's okay."

Trouble is I get wildly excited and want Bob to react in exactly the same manner as myself. He's much more matter-of-fact, and sometimes that leaves me feeling flat.

That time I decided Bob simply wasn't going to scream and shout as I thought he should, so I kissed him, took the check, and scooted!

It was exciting to learn that my dad, who rededicated his life to Jesus when we visited him in Sasakwa, Oklahoma after Bob's illness, had been working on a special gift idea, too. Dad and his wife, Jewel, helped purchase a bus for their church in Oklahoma.

Bob's obedience to the Lord meant we would have to delay beginning the addition to our house by a month or longer. We didn't know exactly when the money would come in, but it was as if God were saying, "Which comes first, My work or your home? Can't you trust Me to provide?"

By February He had provided, and work on our new wing began.

What's more, one of our big clients decided this year would be the one to raise my fee—the first raise in five years. Would you believe the increase was *double* what we gave Jesus?

And would you believe some extra bookings came from out of the blue, and *tripled* the amount we had given to the church?

Kathy Higley, who was the twins' nursemaid when we decided to forgo the addition, in order to tithe, wrote, "Thanks for reminding me of God's provision," when she heard we had begun to build. "It reminded me that once we turn over something to the Lord, very often He will turn around and give us the very thing we gave up."

I'd like to write in big, bold letters every Christian could see: YOU CAN'T OUTGIVE GOD. And when God speaks to us and tells us to give a certain amount, I think we each should pray hard before we decide we "can't afford it."

When you see the Lord work money miracles that way, it humbles you. It helps overcome those times when I get the spending fever and just want to buy impulsively, like a child in a candy store.

God has shown me that when I *really* want to buy a certain thing, but feel Him check me, the thing to do is wait. Don't buy. Later, if I still want the item and feel peace in my heart, it's okay to buy it. I'm learning that if I wait, I usually don't want to go back and make the purchase.

I also asked Phil Braunstein to put me on a clothing budget to allow me to learn to stay within it, instead of going to Bob and asking for every little thing.

In doing battle with submission, I somehow got the

warped idea that Bob must approve of everything I bought or spent or did. It was as though I was seeking God's approval of me through Bob's eyes.

Eventually I realized that neither God nor Bob required all this checking on me, but I simply wanted me to do what I knew was right.

The God in you should be able to guide you in ordering groceries economically and help you not to yield to the temptation to buy your children the most expensive party clothes or buy yourself a new outfit you really don't need.

The Lord is the best teacher, but Bob is working with me, too. (Bob calls me a shoe freak because of the shoes in my closet, some of which are fifteen years old, which I refused to part with.) It may all sound superficial, but it isn't; there are very deep issues here. The excess of shoes in my closet today harks back to the insecure little girl I used to be, fighting to get ahead in the professional world, frightened that the clothes I needed might not be forthcoming, and determined that *someday* I would be a star with all the right clothes for my public appearances.

God understands us, through and through. He heals and forgives and helps us grow up.

My friend Charlotte Topping, who was widowed two years ago when her husband, New York Yankees owner Dan Topping, died, has done so much to inspire me to learn how to handle money. Charlotte inherited some awesome responsibilities with her husband's estate. Dealing with lawyers and executors, learning many lessons the hard way, she had to struggle alone. She'd had no experience with money, and suddenly had to learn how to cope.

Charlotte urges every woman to learn to budget and to acquaint herself with all the details of family business matters. Now. *Today*. Tomorrow may be too late, and a grieving person has no heart for taking on the cold facts of financial life at a time like that.

Women, let the Lord show you where you might fall short when it comes to a healthy approach to money and its capacities. And men, surely the Lord holds you responsible for *knowing* your wife can handle money wisely—and having the children learn how. And in homes where the wife handles the finances, it is just as important that the husband understand them also.

I cannot overstress the importance of our learning monetary self-control. God warns us in 1 Timothy 6:9–11:

> But they that will be rich fall into temptation and a snare, and into many foolish and hurtful lusts, which drown men in destruction and perdition.
>
> For the love of money is the root of all evil: which while some coveted after, they have erred from the faith, and pierced themselves through with many sorrows.
>
> But thou, O man of God, flee these things; and follow after righteousness, godliness, faith, love, patience, meekness.

God supplies. He trains us where we are ignorant. He forgives us where we are wrong. He heals us, deep in our inner selves, where we are broken.

Jesus Himself came to show us the way to our own particular maturity. In Matthew 6:33 He urges us, "But seek ye first the kingdom of God, and his righteousness; and all these things shall be added unto you."

Amen and amen!

Anita

9

Heritage of the Lord

> Lo, CHILDREN are an heritage of the Lord: and the fruit
> of the womb is His reward.
>
> Psalms 127:3

I had started praying, "Lord, teach me submission to Bob."
I also prayed, "Lord, teach me to be poured out wine and
broken bread for my family." I really wanted that, and I
wanted to learn from the perfect Teacher, the Holy Spirit.

I asked God to show me the children's deepest needs and
to help me meet them in some unique way I'd never known
before. "I really want to minister to them," I told Him.
("Boy," as Grandma Berry used to say, "be careful what
you pray for; you may get it!")

As you pray for your children, God reveals to a mother
the specific areas of their lives that He is working on. You
find yourself trying to silently cooperate with the Lord in
the rearing of that child.

It's really exciting. For example, the Lord gave me an insight that Gloria, who is shy about revealing her feelings,
had deep needs she wasn't expressing and that weren't being

met. Gloria never will push and shove for attention, and He showed me that.

So I tried to do some special things with Gloria, to make myself more available to her and to share with her in a spiritual way. The change in our relationship is beautiful. She's quite a talented girl—a good little pianist, especially—and it would be easy to focus on Gloria's attainments and fail to pay enough attention to *her*.

One day Gloria came to me requesting permission to audition for *Sound of Music* which was to be sponsored by the Miami Beach Music and Arts League and held in the Theatre of the Performing Arts. I couldn't believe my ears: was this Gloria, my shy one?

I also felt very real dismay. I had never faced the question of what we would do if one of our kids seemed interested in show business. I told Gloria we would have to check out the production before we could even allow her to audition. As I questioned her, it developed that two of her best friends at school—Sarah McKinnon and Donna Harris —wanted to audition. Maybe they talked her into it, I thought.

"Gloria, why do you want to do this?" I asked.

"I think it would be fun."

Oh, well, she won't get the part, I thought. What are you so worried about? So I made a phone call or two about the production, and it checked out fine. We allowed Gloria to audition.

Meanwhile, deep inside me, I felt so many emotions which I couldn't do anything about. "Lord, please don't let this be the beginning of anything," I prayed.

What can you do when you feel so uncertain, but pray

and turn it over to the Lord? "Dear God, if this isn't part of Your blueprint for Gloria's life, please just close that door before it even opens," I asked.

No matter how it turned out, I determined I would be submissive to the Lord. Gloria auditioned for the part of Marta. Even when she made it to the final auditions, I still doubted that she would actually be chosen; so I didn't worry. So when Gloria *was* chosen, I felt flabbergasted!

A few days later Barbara telephoned from school saying, "Mommie, I want a part in *Sound of Music.*"

"That's too bad. It's too late for you to try out," I told her, gratefully. "They've chosen someone for Gretel's part by now."

"No, Mommie. The man came to school today and picked me and asked me to sing for him."

"Sing for him?" I echoed stupidly.

"Yes, Mommie. So I did, and I think I got the part."

"Got the part?" I yelled. "What do you mean, you think you got the part?"

"I *really* want to do it, Mommie," she said in a determined little voice. "May I, *please?*"

Now I *really* felt agitated—and more than a little suspicious about the choice of my two children for this production. The more I thought about it, the more convinced I became that Gloria and Barbara must have been chosen because they are Anita Bryant's daughters—and that made me irate.

At last I did the only thing I could do—I phoned the show's producer and leveled with him. "Gloria and Barbara were selected on a talent basis," he assured me. "Remember, I have too much at stake myself to play any games. I chose your girls because I think they can handle their roles."

Thus began several weeks of pure hassle. The show was scheduled for one night only, and there were absolutely no tickets available. What's more, the show was plagued with problems. Several times I wanted to pull the girls out, but they would beg, "No Mommie, we want to do it."

Rehearsals often went two or three hours overtime. The kids didn't eat right, bedtime went out the window, and I began to think this was the biggest mistake of my maternal career. Gloria began having trouble in school, and then both girls caught the flu and almost didn't get to be in the show.

Our whole household became thoroughly disrupted by the daily rehearsal schedule. Bob became especially vocal about all the hassle, especially the unpredictable mealtimes, and he really wanted to take the girls out. But soon it was too late; the show had gone past the point where anyone could give up a part. The girls would have to live up to what they had promised.

It was hard getting the girls to and from rehearsals since the schedule Bob and I had called for us to be out of town often. I was especially grateful to Florence Glist, the mother of Stewart who was also in the production. If she had not been there to act like the mother hen to all the kids when I wasn't there, I wouldn't have let the girls continue.

After weeks of desperate, spiraling strain on one and all, the big night arrived. *Sound of Music* is a great musical, and this performance featured a fantastically talented cast. Each of the performers was marvelous, but the children in particular stole the show. (Does this sound like a boasting parent?)

Mother flew in for the performance, and I did something I said I would never do—pull rank to get tickets. Mother and I were backstage hemming costumes and making up the girls, plus worrying about Gloria and Barbara, and we barely had time to rush out and get our seats and enjoy the show.

Our kids amazed us. They really had worked hard, and they really gave to the audience. I found myself so touched and stirred, watching our girls as they played their hearts out, but Bob was really funny. People would be responding to his daughters, but he'd shrug it off and say something to downplay the whole thing, when all the time his face gave him away. He was grinning all over, proud as punch, and so was our dear friend Jody Dunton.

Bobby and Billy couldn't believe how well their sisters did. Afterwards they told them, "You were really cute."

Farmor and Mother sat together, and of course, all they could talk about was their cute granddaughters on the stage. When the people around them kept oohing and aahing over the girls, they both kept turning around and saying, "That's my granddaughter."

This was the first time in my life that I was on the assisting end of things; always before, others had helped me. It gave me a feeling to see how demanding my own life must have been on Mother.

Our girls, through *Sound of Music,* gained a new respect for me. This was the first time they had any conception of how hard I work.

Speaking of rehearsals, they said, "Mommie, you did *Sound of Music* sixty times?"

"Mommie played Maria's role," I told them. "Plus, every week or so we changed theaters. That meant rehearsals all over again!"

Thus I had an opportunity to share with the girls some things they had never known before or had any reason to know. For example, when I saw Gloria was serious about her part, I said, "If you're really sincere about this, let me show you how to breathe properly."

After a couple of lessons, she told me, "That's hard."

"It is hard at first," I told her, "but this is part of the important discipline of show business. It's fun, but it's hard."

Barbara, who normally strongly projects her voice around the house, became shy during the rehearsals. I think she was scared of the director. But I was able to prod her to project by saying in order for the audience to hear, you will have to really yell out your lines. The night of the performance, she really projected and was so cute. Gloria did the best acting in the show and Barbara, of course, had the lines that stole the show.

Maybe all the hard work and hassle were worthwhile for the girls and the rest of us. They did get a glimpse into my world, and their own hard work on *Sound of Music* obviously increased their respect for my hard work. For the first time I became aware that it is important for boys and girls to become aware of just *how* their parents earn a living.

Our kids definitely notice that Bob and I get turned-on by our work. It's a continuous stimulation and challenge. There's always something new to learn, or something old to improve.

They also notice that their parents read a lot. Bob always has a newspaper or news magazine in his hand, and I'm always sure to read any new good Christian books. The Bible says, "Train up a child in the way he should go: and when he is old, he will not depart from it" (Proverbs 22:6). Mental discipline is so important, and we believe in setting an example of good reading habits instead of just nagging our kids to read.

What's more, I'm building a library for each child. As I encounter books that minister to me, I buy copies for each one, and I write notes to them along the way. These libraries include various versions of the Holy Bible, all of their parents' books, plus many others I want them to own. We're trying to train our children to seek out understanding. The reading habit is something they *catch* from parents who love to read, we believe.

The Bible says, "Even a child is known by his doings, whether his work be pure and whether it be right" (Proverbs 20:11). As parents, Bob and I know we can insist on rules being kept and work being done and obedience maintained, but only the Holy Spirit of God can instill in these children real love for one another.

Like all children, they're difficult at times—pesky or hot-tempered or argumentative—and it seems they're always testing us. But they are good people. More and more I feel the need to minister to each of them through daily prayer. I lift each one to the Lord so many, many times during the day.

And sometimes they throw you a curve, such as the time Gloria signed up for a schook track meet and failed to tell us until the last minute. We needed that Saturday for the

family; so I felt myself getting irritated. I had to phone the
school to learn the times of Gloria's events, and that made it
worse: she was to run the hundred-yard dash at 9:00 A.M.,
the triple jump at 12:30 P.M., and the 220 at 3:00 P.M.

Bob couldn't help because Bobby needed him for some
special project. Also, I needed the Saturday off and felt it
unfair that I should have to get up early on Saturday morning to chauffeur Gloria.

But beyond that, I felt Gloria needed the family there to
cheer her on. The whole thing began to sound like bad news.
Even when Barbara decided to go with us, I still felt put
out. Then Bob suggested that Gloria might skip the first
event and run the second two, so we wouldn't have to sit
there all day.

"Okay," she decided somewhat reluctantly. "I just told
them I'd be there Saturday; I didn't tell them I'd be there
for all three."

I thought Bob's suggestion was a bad idea. Gloria had
committed herself for three events, and I thought it wasn't
right to encourage her to cop out on the first one. Also, we
want the kids to do these extracurricular sports; so it
seemed wrong to take this opportunity so lightly.

So, because I really didn't want to get up that early, I
gave in to Bob's suggestion. We arrived at school at 11:30,
an hour early, only to learn that a number of other kids
hadn't shown up, and several events had to be canceled.
That moved the schedule up so Gloria had missed, not only
her first event, but also the second one as well.

Wow! I was mad at Bob and even more mad at myself. I
had to tell Gloria's teacher it was our fault that she missed

her first two meets. She did run the third one, and came in second place.

Disappointed, disgusted, and chagrined, I attempted, as we drove home, to explain to my daughter: "Gloria, from now on when you enter an event, you must consider the whole family and ask Mommie and Daddy so we can be sure to coordinate with you. We want to back you up.

"But this is a good lesson for you and me: that when we promise to do something, we must live up to our word and not be irresponsible. Just because other people don't show up. . . ."

I also promised myself that henceforth, even if she did make an inconvenient commitment, I would put myself out and get her there. I want her to know how important it is to keep your word, even at great personal inconvenience.

Kids have to learn about the gray areas of life—that everything isn't just black and white. I explained that Daddy was trying to think of everybody's needs that day, including my need to sleep in; so he was suggesting a compromise. As it turned out, I didn't agree it was a good compromise because it left Gloria with egg on her face, unable to say a thing except "I was irresponsible and didn't do what I said I would."

In the long run, despite the fiasco, Gloria and Daddy and Mommie learned a good lesson. It made the point that when one agrees to something, he must think of the effect on the rest of the family. We must consider the family as a whole, and the whole family in turn must consider the individual's needs as they arise.

Billy and Barbara are quite athletically inclined. Barbara suffered a slight touch of cerebral palsy at birth which resulted in tight tendons in the back of her legs. We gave her ballet lessons, and she's doing fine. Barbara reminds me of myself, especially since she is hardheaded and has a mind of her own. She loves to spend hours in the nursery playing my records and singing along, which is what I used to do when I was her age.

Billy always has been well coordinated despite the fact that as a child he was terribly bowlegged and had to wear casts and corrective shoes. As an infant, Billy had undergone surgery for hammertoes, and even before that, he had been operated on for a double hernia when brand-new and weighing only five pounds.

Both learned to swim at age three, and they're snow and waterskiing now. Barbara is somewhat behind Billy physically, but her mind amazes us—and sometimes she centers that power of concentration onto some new physical challenge and surprises all of us.

Many times when I give my testimony and tell about the twins, I skim over one of the greatest miracles—that Barbara survived without brain damage. She had such a difficult start in life, even more so than her twin, and nowadays when we see them running, swimming, climbing, or laughing together, Bob and I say, "Thank You, Jesus." And when we look at Barbara, we're reminded that she not only escaped brain damage but actually has superior intelligence, which definitely is a gift of the Lord. Praise God!

Our older children are entering adolescence. Bobby, as always, is tremendously independent but wants and needs much affection. Gloria is quiet, sensitive, and still clings to her parents a bit. Billy and Barbara are funny, independent, and healthy.

So, it's a four-ring circus around here. I keep the prayers going, try to appreciate each child for himself, and realize that God is at work on those little areas of character or personality weakness we parents observe.

How good that we don't have to rear these children all alone—that our God, the perfect Parent, is molding and shaping these little ones even when their imperfect human parents make mistakes!

In teaching your children how to run the good race, we parents have to set the example. We're trying to get them to see that everything they do has consequences—that they're to do everything "as unto the Lord." That's when you get down to the nitty-gritty, especially when you discover you need to change some of your own habits.

In seeking God's will for feeding my family, He first brought me face-to-face with myself. I've always been one who could take food or leave it, and I had developed a real snack pattern. Even when I saw that the children ate good, balanced meals, I stayed pretty indifferent about how I ate. Then I started reading up on nutrition and became aware of how I was shortchanging myself.

Evelyn Galvin, a Christian friend I really respect, inspired me to learn effective diet and nutrition habits, and to add natural vitamins to our family's routine. Three years ago, Evelyn was the catalyst for Time of Renewal, a thrilling workshop for Christian women in which she and Teddy Heard and I, among others, were privileged to minister to several hundred women in our community.

Bill and Evelyn Galvin have become really knowledgeable about nutrition and good health. They set glowing examples of good stewardship before us. They are vital, upbeat Christians, the kind who inspire you to upgrade your own habits.

Bill runs a diagnostic center at the Cedars of Lebanon Hospital in Miami, and Evelyn is working out a beautiful idea for a spa for creating an opportunity for women to experience Christian renewal using the principles of good nutrition and spiritual health.

Negligence about nutrition, I realized, can make kids' school grades go down, and can affect their teeth, hair, eyesight, and their skin quality. I started paying attention to these things, for me, as well as for them.

I've come to believe that a lot of our kids' irritability probably traces back to nutritional lacks. A cranky child often is hungry, and pop and potato chips won't hack it. In line with that, I read somewhere that certain foods quiet the nervous individual as effectively as three aspirin tablets or even a tranquilizer and that they naturally create a sense of well-being. I don't know about that; I can't evaluate the statement scientifically, but I do believe many people run around hungry much of the time!

We're developing new food habits at our house. We're serving cheese and crackers, fresh fruits, milk, and juices, including more Florida orange juice, instead of the junk foods they love. We've had far less grumbling than I expected. Bob and I are surprised at how well they accepted the change of pace.

Naturally they love ice cream, but there's almost no cooky-jar-and-ice-cream-after-every-meal routine around here any more. Parties are the exception; they can go the whole route, including candy and soda pop. That makes those foods special, and they enjoy them more when they're not everyday affairs.

I plan my menus once a week and build in plenty of variety. We eat a lot of chicken and fish in addition to beef. Occasionally I throw in something they're not used to eating—a new casserole or breakfast food—just to get them to try new things.

Gloria loves yogurt, and often on Saturdays, she chooses that for lunch. She loves food and is a good cook, but she also knows she has to watch it. Like Bob, she could become a foodaholic. Sometimes she says, "Mommie, may I have a little ice cream?" and I say, "If you want to get fat." And then we laugh.

Gloria thinks it over and decides for herself. The point is she *thinks,* and when she really wants ice cream, she eats it without guilt, especially after she has exercised a lot. At age twelve Gloria is learning to control her life. She wants to have a good figure; so she has learned what to eat.

Bob and I want her to like herself and feel good about herself, and that's what happens when a child or an adult exercises self-control. But we parents set the pace. The kids respect Bob for fighting his weight problem. They really try to help him.

Friday nights, which are our relaxed family evenings, we try to help the children. The kids get to sit up and watch television a little later on Fridays, and I used to let them munch on all sorts of snacks. Now we monitor the eating just as carefully as we monitor the viewing. Barbara and Gloria help me fix trays of fresh fruit, cheeses and crackers, and Florida orange juice or other natural juices.

For a while they protested giving up the junk, but they

soon developed a taste for fruits and cheeses. It's important to remember that kids bend. You can change their habits in these little ways.

I'm also a stickler about sleep. Our kids' biggest complaint is that some of their schoolmates get to stay up until eleven and twelve o'clock at night watching television. Our children don't get to watch TV during the week unless there's an excellent program going, and they get to bed early—much earlier than they want to!

Maybe all this sounds tedious, but Bob and I believe the Lord expects us to instill good, disciplined habits in our children *now*. Each child has responsibilities according to his age, and he's expected to do his chores daily.

Looking about for some way to regulate these duties—I admit we used to have plenty of confusion at times over who did what job—I thought of how God said that they who are wise will lead many righteous to the Lord, and they will shine as the stars forever (*see* Daniel 12:3). And I thought, the star system!

So we posted a chart that has each child's name and daily duties listed. They enjoy pasting up stars when they make their bed, clean up their room, put toys away, eat all their breakfast, take vitamins, feed their pets, and so on. Best of all, each child monitors himself pretty much. I don't continually follow around checking up on them.

They must earn a certain number of stars each day and a certain total on Fridays to stay up and watch TV on Friday night. They can earn bonus stars when they do something extra such as memorizing a Bible verse, practicing piano, or perhaps offering to clear the table.

Virginia Spear, my cousin, came to visit me one morning

out in Oklahoma City where she is with station KRMC. She was sharing with me about the Lord, and during our precious sharing time she gave me a Love Trophy. She explained that each child who displays the most love in a given week, gets the Love Trophy that week and gets to keep the trophy in his room.

In keeping with 1 Corinthians 13, the children are learning to set their wills toward love. When we will to love, the Lord changes our heart and attitude. When I see an attitude of spontaneous kindness expressed by one of the children, he gets the trophy, and it really works. Bobby has worked the hardest and has taken great initiative. Actually, each child is changing noticeably and is really concentrating on learning how Jesus wants us to live.

In addition, the Love Trophy winner gets a special day when they get to do whatever they want with Mommie or Daddy, such as going on a shopping trip or to a special movie. The Love Trophy means a lot to the kids. It's good competition but it also helps establish love attitudes; so chores are done with an attitude of love.

We're trying to encourage good behavior, reward good self-discipline, and teach cooperation. We're aiming toward a positive approach to life rather than a punitive attitude or a *do-this-because-I-say-so* feeling in our home. Bob and I want our children to take responsibility for themselves.

I used to worry about our children's material wealth—worry that it would spoil them and they couldn't handle it. But I've learned that if we uphold God's standards, teach them real self-discipline and self-respect, and if God is disciplining me not to spend excessively, we won't have spoiled children.

God delights in showering His gifts and blessings on His

children, but if He failed to discipline and chastise us, how spoiled we would be—too spoiled to appreciate His ultimate goodness.

Just so with our children. It's not giving them too many things that spoils them necessarily, but failing to teach them discipline and responsibility spoils them. Those are the underprivileged children, no matter how rich their parents may be.

But if you work hard to stay in the will of the Lord, if you take on the hard work of really teaching your children, and if somehow you really lead them to "seek ye first the kingdom of God, and his righteousness" (Matthew 6:33), then they can't be spoiled by things.

We have to let God show us how to develop in our children the kind of character it takes to cope with the world. Above all, we must consider the whole person, and not neglect any area of mind, body, and spirit to which God would have us minister.

One thing that illustrates this principle to me is the joy I felt last Easter. Now I had looked forward to that holiday with all my heart—and then it seemed that I was going to miss it altogether.

For one thing, this would be Farfar's first Easter since he received his salvation. I could hardly wait to see him experience the joy of the whole church when they learned Farfar had accepted Christ. I wanted to share that moment with Bob and the children and wanted to praise God with all my heart for His Son Jesus, who means so much to me.

Bruce and Ann Howe would share that special occasion with us, too. Bruce, who is vice-president of music publishing at Word Records, and Bob are friends of long standing.

The Bible says, ". . . there is a friend that sticketh closer than a brother" (Proverbs 18:24), and their relationship is that way. Bruce and Ann would understand the importance of the day.

But then Billy developed an infected knee after falling down while skating. The knee swelled so badly that we were afraid he might have to go to the hospital. I would have to stay home with Billy that Easter Sunday.

To make matters worse, Farfar stayed with us that weekend, and he had deteriorated so rapidly that we realized he would probably never again be able to be left without supervision. We put him to bed in the Florida room and I slept close by in a sleeping bag on the floor. Meanwhile, I was up and down all night with Billy, giving him regular doses of antibiotics.

When Easter arrived, I had been without sleep for two nights and was so tired I thought I would die. We had planned to enjoy a big family celebration at the Bath Club after church, but I saw I needed to stay home with Farfar and Billy.

At first I really pitied myself or wanted to. I thought it wasn't fair. "Why me, God?" I asked. I also hated to miss being with my Sunday school class of eleven-year-old girls that morning.

What happened? I told God I wanted to submit to His perfect will for me in this messed-up situation. I asked Him to help me to minister to my family and to be willing to put self to one side this time. Especially I asked what to do about dinner. I realized Farfar might be able to exercise self-control throughout the church service, but might not be able to make it through dinner. What to do?

The Lord led me to decide—despite my fatigue—to fix lunch at home for the crowd. I could watch Billy and prepare lunch while the others were in church.

Once my decision had been made, I felt true freedom and joy. The self-pity and resentment evaporated. Then Karen Kinnett, who then worked with Bob as a vice-president for Fishers of Men, offered to stay home and take care of Billy so I could go to church. I felt so tempted! However, I knew it was my responsibility to take care of Billy; so I declined.

Next Bob offered to stay home. I told him he should take his father to church—how eager he was to do it!—and besides, it wasn't his place to stay home with Billy, but mine. I was under God's thumb and knew that even though I didn't like the way things were turning out, I was going to be obedient to Him, and I rejoiced in it.

I arose very early on Easter Sunday before anyone else got up. I made some coffee, got my Bible, and went outside by the bay. I'd had perhaps an hour's sleep all night; yet as I sat there for perhaps ten minutes and read the Easter story aloud to myself, I knew I was experiencing one of the most joyous Easters I had ever known.

I knew I was in the will of the Lord and happy to be serving my family. Maybe I can't minister in any ways the world can see, but the ministry the Lord has placed me in begins in Villa Verde. I just praise Him that I know it and am not resisting or chafing about the nitty-gritty of life.

We got the children ready for church—and Farfar too— and soon everyone departed. As I began to prepare lunch, Karen Kinnett arrived to help me. How good of the Lord and how unselfish of Karen to do that sweet thing! As we flew around, setting the table, fixing vegetables, chatting together over salads and breads and garnishes for the roast lamb, Karen and I praised God and almost held church in our kitchen.

So from the day's beginning, I felt the joy of the Lord. Bob unintentionally wanted to rob me of that joy because he wanted to send out for food. He felt really bad that I couldn't go to church on Easter, he was concerned for my lack of sleep, and he really didn't want me to do any extra work. It was hard for me to convince him that this was something I really wanted to do.

After church we gathered around the long table, all chatting and sharing and enjoying good food and a glorious Easter Sunday. Farfar glowed with happiness. Bob looked totally contented. It was one of those moments that stands out with perfect clarity; I knew I was blessed, knew I was happy, and knew I had received my precious heritage from the Lord.

Praise be to God!

10
To Work and to Witness

AT THE MAYOR'S PRAYER breakfast in Orlando, Florida, one man said to me: "Sir, I'm going to pray for you. You have a big cross to bear, being Anita Bryant's husband and manager."

I'm sure I looked startled at first, not sure of what he meant, but the truth was Anita's sincere testimony about what the Lord has done for us, and what He wants to do for you, had touched this guy deeply. He had received an insight as to what Anita and I are all about—and I, for one, greatly appreciate his prayers.

More and more, the Lord blesses us with opportunities to combine work with witness. Just a few years ago that sort of thing would have been out of the question, but today most of our bookings *request*, not just a concert or personal appearance, but the Christian testimony as well.

Every time we fill a new booking or hit a new town, we pray for opportunities to share Jesus. And wow, do those prayers get answered!

The Bible says:

Whatsoever ye do, do it heartily, as to the Lord, and not
unto men;

Knowing that of the Lord ye shall receive the reward of
the inheritance: for ye serve the Lord Christ.

Colossians 3:23–24

That's our goal—to work as unto the Lord, and for God
to reach lost souls through our work. And the more we try
to combine work and witness, the more God seems to bless
what we're trying to do.

Fishers of Men Opportunities, Inc., my fledgling Christian talent agency, still is striving to break even financially.
The Anita Bryant Singers, our new girls' singing group, are
appearing all over the country—and here again, our goal
with them is to break even. They're not yet paying their
own way, but that's not too important now: Fishers and
ABS are our ministry.

The past two years have proved my contention that
there's a valid place for such a ministry. Fishers of Men has
become a central clearinghouse for artists. We serve the
church, and also serve the needs of the Christian artist or
celebrity who doesn't have time to handle phone calls or to
make decisions on working conditions and setting fees.

We have working arrangements with such people as former Miss America Vonda Van Dyke, Norma Zimmer from
the "Lawrence Welk Show," Alvin Dark, and other top
talents. The Lord is blessing the whole thing.

Meanwhile, as Anita's career continues to mushroom,
more and more the Lord seems to put her on TV talk
shows. Usually they don't want her to talk about her faith

or do any more than mention our books; yet they'll turn around and ask questions that give her the perfect opening.

Merv Griffin, for example, asked, "I never realized when you first got into show business that you were this religious. What happened?" That gave Anita the perfect lead-in to say: "When I was eight years old, I promised myself I was going to be a star. Then I met the Creator of stars, and I invited Jesus Christ into my heart." Then she gave her testimony.

Another host said, "I understand you had a nervous breakdown." That remark might have thrown another performer, but Anita praised God. "He wouldn't have known that, most likely, unless he read *Light My Candle*," she told me.

Then came the "Mike Douglas Show," the first network show ever to come into Disney World. The Florida Citrus Commission voted to sponsor it with the stipulation that Mike allow Anita to cohost the show. It was a ticklish situation, despite Anita's long-standing friendship and professional relationship with Mike, because there appeared to be some resistance to her strong stand for Jesus Christ.

We wondered if they would take the Florida Citrus Commission up on their offer. If she can do the show without talking about Jesus, she can do it was the verdict. Our sponsor wanted her to do the show, but we realized she'd be expected to cool the testimony and appear as an entertainer only.

We really prayed about it. We realized our decision, whichever way it went, would set a precedent. We also expected God to take the situation and work it into something good. We claimed Romans 8:28 which says:

. . . all things work together for good to them that love God, to them who are called according to his purpose.

After considerable prayer, Anita decided this was a time God wanted her to practice submission; she would present a silent witness. "God made Anita Bryant, the performer, as well as Anita Bryant, the Christian, and His word says He will never leave me or forsake me," she told me.

Meanwhile everything turned to bedlam at home. My mom couldn't help with the kids because of Dad, and we couldn't find anyone competent to stay with them for that week. Satan really tried to get in there and mess things up.

That is when Karen Kinnett, who is a wonderful Christian gal and very mature for her age, appeared on the scene. We stepped out on faith and left her in charge of our four kids. Anita felt somewhat nervous, but she needed me during that hectic week of shooting. The show was set up like a travelogue, and they went from scene to scene which was really difficult and hectic with shooting night and day. Anita used ten suitcases of clothes.

All week long, Anita had to deal with her feelings about staying in her place and not verbally witnessing for the Lord. At one point she felt really bad and prayed way into the night. The very next day the Lord sent two Christians to the show—Dean Jones, the famous Disney actor, and his wife Lori. Dean walked up to Anita and said, "Hello, Sister." She did a double take, looked at him funny, and said, "What did you say?"

Dean broke into a big grin and said, "Praise the Lord!"

Then Anita threw her arms around him and yelled, "Boy, am I glad to see you!"

The rest of the week was super. We were able to spend time fellowshiping with and getting to know Lori and Dean. The show worked well, we liked the crew, and they liked us, and we ended up giving copies of our books to several members. Anita decided the Lord had blessed our submission; and we agreed that in the end, He did allow us to witness—through love, peace, and joy.

Professionally speaking, the show undoubtedly was one of the best Anita ever did. It was great fun, and we had a ball. The Lord kept our sense of humor going; so maybe they realized Christians are human after all, that we can keep up with them in any given situation. Maybe that helps break down barriers between those who love the Lord and those who don't know Him yet.

As we travel the country's small towns, we're struck once more by the feeling that small-town Americans are the real strength of this country. You look out into a rural audience and feel so impressed by the clean, strong faces.

While doing a performance in Hattiesburg, Mississippi, where William Carey gave Anita her first honorary doctorate degree—Doctor of Humane Letters—we became friends with Ollie and John Thomas. Ollie was head of the cancer campaign there for which we did the show. Arrangements had been made for Ollie and John to meet us in New Orleans with their private plane. Failure of a mechanical part prevented this and John was upset and frustrated. Anita told him to "Praise the Lord anyway," and he declared he was going to have new lettering put on the side of the aircraft: PRAISE THE LORD ANYWAY!

Also, when we did a July 4 show in Ruston, Louisiana, we were so grateful to Diane and James Davison and their four children. They did so much for us during those four shows, and we feel we have gained them as close friends.

We stayed with Fran and Bill Terry on their beautiful farm in Lexington, Kentucky, when Anita did a show for their new Coca-Cola bottling plant there. Gloria and Bobby had a wonderful time horseback riding and we were so grateful for the friendship of Fran and Bill.

In July Anita had a chance to perform in Tulsa for the first time since 1962. Some six thousand people showed up for the launching of the new Heritage Baptist Church with the Reverend Mark Smith as pastor, among them numerous members of Anita's family. Her mother and Daddy George, Uncle Luther Berry and Aunt Marie, Cousins Wendell and Patsy Critenden and their son Bryan and daughter Melody, Covil and Marguerite Page, parents of my brother-in-law Sam Page, Anita's Aunt Betty and her husband Bob Callen and their daughter Cindy were there, as well as our friend, Julie Twilley.

It was like a family reunion. After the show we had dinner together and then a big sharing time at Julie's house. Anita told how she had offended some people by doing a dancing and baton twirling sequence on the Stars and Stripes Show, resulting in a future booking being canceled.

We really prayed about that. Anita had borrowed a baton twirler's costume and did the routine—and the drill team on the show really related to her. They came to her and asked her to lead a prayer service that Sunday morning since there wasn't time to go to church. The team, called the

Coogans, are all committed, born-again Christians. They all gathered around to hear Anita give a Sunday school lesson, share a bit of her testimony, and sing a couple of songs. Other cast members were there too, including Barbara Peterson—Miss U.S.A., Deana Jo Harrogarra—Miss American Indian, Katherine Durden—the new Miss Teenage America, and Lenne Jo Hallgren—America's Junior Miss.

Barbara is extremely interested in our Fishers of Men talent and booking agency and is seriously considering becoming part of it in the very near future. She would be excellent especially for speaking engagements and public relations.

Later, three of the gals told Anita she led them to rededicate their lives to Christ.

In sharing those things, Anita's Aunt Marie, who is a pastor's wife, spoke up and told about those times when Christians make a point of not preaching or even talking about the Lord. Anita's Uncle Luther calls it *cultivating*—fellowshiping, getting to know people, or preparing the soil of faith.

Uncle Luther says there's a time to be a visual witness, instead of a verbal witness. He advises us to be lovable, attractive *human beings*—and leave the rest to the Lord. There's a time to quietly cultivate as well as a time to be verbal, depending on the situation, Uncle Luther says. I think there's a lot to what he says.

We did a ski commercial in Sun Valley and, of course, had a fantastic time. But Anita and I came away with a great concern for the young people on the slopes out there. Jim Irwin and others familiar with the ski scene compare it to the surfers. We met such superintelligent, keen young people on the slopes, but their god is skiing.

I've never seen an area so void of religion as that scene. We had never been in another area of the U.S. where for two weeks we found no mention of faith. Here we encountered a total void.

Maybe someday Fishers of Men can sponsor some dynamic Christian young people who are into skiing and can take the Bible to the slopes. Hopefully we can send people, who not only enjoy what God gave us in terms of mountains, weather, skiing thrills, and all that, but who also can share what God gave us in terms of His Son. The slopes are a mission field.

One night, as Anita spoke to forty-thousand people in the Houston Civic Center, she found herself speaking to America's need for prayer—how it's not the world that needs changing, but people, and how only God can get to the heart of our problems and change us as individuals.

"What we really need to do is get down on our knees and do some good, old-fashioned praying," she said.

Several weeks later Chuck Bird, our conductor-arranger, woke up at three in the morning with this line on his mind, and in about twenty minutes, he wrote a song called "Old-Fashioned Praying."

Chuck never brags about his talent, but a few days later he came over. "I'm going to play your next hit record for you," he told Anita. When she heard it, she said, "That's one of the best songs I've heard in a long time." It's a super song. It says so much about the needs our country must get back to, and where we are right now. It has a contemporary beat, and it's up-to-the-minute.

Anita debuted the song during the Junior Orange Bowl Parade this year. We believe God gave Chuck the inspiration, and we feel this record is something special, even for Anita.

We also did a Bicentennial convention for Amoco. Anita doesn't play Las Vegas, but they did a very fine show, featuring Anita and the Anita Bryant Singers in several sacred and patriotic numbers. They wanted her testimony, too. It was an ideal show, from our point of view, and one of the best in her career.

We performed in the mornings for America's oil jobbers in the very spot where Dean Martin was packing people in at night. What a contrast!

Out of this engagement came an outpouring of beautiful letters from Amoco people. We really appreciated these reactions. We also appreciated a fellow named Pat, who worked the spotlight and came backstage to tell us he's a Christian and thinks it's great to be able to work with other Christians in show business.

These are just a few highlights of a fantastic new phase of life God seems to be bringing us into. When we first brought our work and our witness together, we were a little hesitant about it. Now, however, the more we step out on faith, the more He blesses us.

Sometimes when you are physically exhausted and have absolutely nothing left to give, God can use you best. Several months ago Anita and I made the forty-five minute trip from Lakeland, Florida to Orlando. We had worked hard and late the night before, and hired a limousine to get us to the airport for an early flight home. Nobody felt like talking, believe me, yet God initiated a conversation between the driver and us. I don't remember how it got started, but tired as we were, we found ourselves roused and witnessing for Jesus. Jim Apthorpe, the driver, an interesting fellow who meets many celebrities in his business, really listened to Anita. Eventually she led him in the sinner's prayer, and he accepted Jesus.

The thing is years earlier a teacher in Jim Apthorpe's public high school had first planted the seed for his conversion. He told us all about Miss Bess Kahout, who never had taught him but who had taken an interest in Jim anyhow. "Ironically, my greatest influence in school was this teacher I never had classes with," he told us.

Jim keeps a celebrity notebook album. These days as he meets all kinds of people in his work, he shows them the album and tells about meeting Anita and receiving his salvation.

He wrote to Miss Kahout and told her about being saved. She told a WCTU meeting about Anita, about Jim's salvation, and about his "limousine album ministry." Miss Kahout helped Jim begin a serious study of the Bible and he keeps us posted on his progress. This has been a great lesson for us. By allowing God to use us when we felt dead tired, we were blessed by seeing someone come to Jesus. Jim in turn witnesses daily and now is helping win souls himself.

More and more, as we travel about the country, we meet other Christians with this same burden for lost souls. We pray the number will increase. As Paul wrote to the Corinthians (1 Corinthians 15:58):

Therefore, my beloved brethren, be ye stedfast, unmoveable, always abounding in the work of the Lord, forasmuch as ye know that your labour is not in vain in the Lord.

Amen!

Anita

11

Dare to Rejoice!

"REJOICE EVERMORE." That's in the Bible (1 Thessalonians 5:16), but I used to read right over it.

Throughout the Bible we're told to rejoice, lift up our hearts, and praise the Lord. So why are there so many unhappy Christians? I know what I'm talking about—I was one of them. I still could be if I let myself.

It's easy to succumb to "not feeling good." People who don't feel good cop out in one way or another, and we've all done that. Our alternative is to learn how to call on God's promises and learn how to live above our circumstances. Yes, we can *learn* to put on the whole armor of God!

But so many people stay inside their houses in their same old ruts with their old ways of thinking. God says, "Behold, I make all things new" (Revelation 21:5). Fantastic! But we're so reluctant to let Him change anything about us.

For example, how long since you learned to do something new—especially something hard? How about night courses, Bible classes, tennis lessons, bike riding, learning to paint or sew or cook—anything to challenge your mind.

The Lord has shown me how much people pick up the vibrations you're giving out in your attitude toward your husband and your family and toward what's happening. They pick up those vibes much quicker than they do your words. If you have right attitudes in your heart—or repressed anger, unhappiness, or animosity—it eventually will spill out of your mouth. They'll pick it up in the atmosphere around you, and that makes you unattractive.

Why should an unbeliever be attracted to that kind of Christian? And yet, we've all known sad-appearing Christians. As a child, I thought Christians never had any fun. I loved to dance, but I grew up in a *thou-shalt-not* sort of strictness which the church, thank goodness, de-emphasizes these days. We're concentrating more on what God *is*, instead of loading people with guilt about frivolity and so on.

Billy Graham says the Christian home should be a happy, laugh-filled place, with plenty of optimism and good things going on for each family member. This is not easy to accomplish, especially today when the family seems to go off in many different directions.

I've been guilty of barking orders like a top sergeant, trying to get everybody else doing whatever he or she should be doing.

The mother sets the tone, which is why I get up early and have my quiet time with the Lord. I know if I'm cranky and grouchy and tense, it is conveyed to Bob and the children, and they each leave home apt to act up on the job or in the classroom, which would be a terrible witness! All of us gals know how that works—vibrations right on down the line.

That's why the woman must be the first to submit to God. Only then can she minister to her husband and children and meet all the other demands. If you submit to God, stay confessed and prayed up, and praise the Lord, you become willing to do whatever He wants you to do. You're in the right attitude to take all the garbage that life sometimes throws at us.

It's hard for my family to adapt to my professional needs, even when they try. After a performance Bob often says for me to sleep and he will get the kids off to school, but I don't expect everyone's schedule to conform to mine. I just have to grab that catch-up sleep whenever I can, and Bob tries to help.

We want a complete family around the breakfast table. We both want to guide our children and are willing to sacrifice personal comfort to do it. Even when you're dead tired and don't think you're being much of a mommie, the kids appreciate your trying.

I used to get down-hearted about this. The Lord has helped me to accept myself as a professional person, and not to punish myself for being who I am. The devil loves to use guilt feelings against us—especially us working mothers, you know.

It's hard for a woman to rejoice when her husband is not in tune with her needs. When I had my emotional breakup, Bob and I learned a lot about that—the main thing was my learning to allow Bob to do more for me. I didn't know how to let go and allow Bob to be the burden bearer he really wants to be—which is a good parallel to the way a lot of us Christians treat God. He wants to help us, wants to bear our burdens, but we just won't turn loose!

I really sold Bob short by not trusting him in these ways— though I didn't recognize it as a lack of trust, of course. Some women tend to be too self-sufficient, don't we, girls! These days I say it in words when it comes to talking about household and child-rearing problems. I used to wait until I got overloaded, then I would blow an emotional fuse. Now I wait until the right time—when Bob is rested, well fed, and ready to talk—then we discuss our nitty-gritty problems constructively.

We're learning to discuss instead of argue, which is hard work. We're also learning how to fight; or rather, how to not-fight. I'm someone who flares up and dumps out anything I want to say, the whole bag of garbage. Bob, on the other hand, harbors things I think he should spit out. What a terrible combination!

The Lord is teaching Bob not to sit on his feelings, but to spit them out—which for him is almost like pulling teeth. God also is teaching me not to say the hot words that want to tumble out, but to wait. If it really needs saying, it will wait. Later it comes out kindly, a truth spoken decently and in order, rather than a challenging statement designed to get my husband. Now, that's the Lord!

It amazes me because I've never had the ability to hold off before. God teaches us "impulsives" self-control, if we let him. I can rejoice over that!

When doing things with love, that man catches more your attitude or vibrations without your saying anything. Same with the kids. When they come home pushy and quarrelsome, instead of lighting into them, figure they've probably had some problem come up in their day and they're frustrated. When you say, "Had a rough day at school, huh?" and encourage them to talk, that often fixes things.

These days I make a point of saying "I love you" each day to Bob and the children. Maybe that comes automatically to you, or maybe not, according to how much affection was expressed in your childhood home—but it's important. For one thing, it means you make a point of taking that little moment of time for each individual. I read the other day that some fathers spend as little as *thirty seconds a day* with their children. How much real time does a mommie take, I wonder?

For years I didn't dare rejoice. I was terribly self-centered and had an enormous guilt complex as well. The superconscientious, perfectionistic sort of person I was simply can't win. Bob constantly said, "You're never happy," and it was true.

I could not begin to mature and heal emotionally until I could recognize my own sin nature, that I had kept self on the throne. I had to learn to accept myself—and to accept Bob—which included strengths and weaknesses, the whole package just as each of us really is. The moment I could admit Bob had some imperfections, I could begin to love him better.

I can see Bob's faults and recognize them, but they're not my problem. Before, his faults made me unhappy and miserable, and I'd react—often with anger—to any remark he threw out. Bob wasn't supposed to have faults, that's all!

God says we're to strengthen one another. We're learning how to speak to one another in love without anyone getting mad or hurt, without losing our kindness and objectivity. That is quite a contrast to the old stormy scenes! We're responding to the healthy side of one another instead of the unhealthy.

All these little snares I've mentioned are so commonplace, but they're still real pitfalls in the paths of Christian progress. We stumble over the small things far more often than anything big.

One trait that robs us of joy is the inability to relax and show the world our fun side. That's a problem with me. Bob often says, "I don't think you had a childhood."

So I'm trying to learn to let my carefree child out as often as possible. Bob has a wonderful ability to be a carefree child with the kids, and so does Farmor. They can get down and play as joyously as any child.

Christians should be the world's beautiful people, radiant inside and out. We should look attractive. Are we as good-looking as God made us? I don't think most Americans are.

Sadly enough, Christians in particular often fall short. And how can we obey God and "rejoice evermore" if we look a mess! Christians should be beautiful as well as happy, with upbeat personalities that come from praising God in all things, with optimism that comes from faith, and with joy that springs from healthy minds and bodies and an outlook of confidence in God.

Before I received emotional treatment, anything could get at me. Now it's like floating on God's stream, being borne along on His current.

Things can still get to you, but you know you are safe in His care. You still get frustrated, depressed, and angry at times, for sure, but over all, there's a power and a strength, and you know where to turn and how to pray, "Restore unto me the joy of thy salvation" (Psalms 51:12).

You know if you wake up one day and don't take time for devotions and communion with your Lord, well, you know what's wrong. You start over. You say, "Lord, I blew it. I know how much You love me. Please take me back again."

In that stream of the Spirit, sometimes you're wading in the shallow water, sometimes deep, and other times in the rocky edge along the banks, but you're never totally out of the life-giving flow.

I'm in awe when I think of how God will take over our lives. My schedule is three times heavier than ever before. I've always worked hard, but this is ridiculous. And at home, everything has become more complicated. We have two dogs, two cats, two birds, two adolescents, not to mention the twins. No wonder things jump around here. But there's a flow now.

You know when you're on a different plateau. You'll never return to that scattered way of life with all its anxieties.

I'm thinking of the Dogwood Arts Festival in Knoxville, Tennessee. That is where we met Kathy Bresee who later came to help with the kids during the summer and was a real blessing. That morning we opened with a prayer breakfast, with songs and testimony, and really giving out for the Lord—a tremendous emotional experience.

Bill Felton and Lynda Kennedy, on behalf of the Dogwood Arts Festival, presented us with a very beautiful—and very special—original watercolor by Barbara Underwood.

Then came the festival parade, and that night, a show. That was a heavy day, you must admit, and when it was over, I felt physically exhausted—yet totally calm and filled with unspeakable joy inside, feeling totally fulfilled as a Christian, a human being, and a performer.

Where does the strength come from? The Lord, of

course. "The joy of the LORD is your strength" (Nehemiah 8:10). It's a whole new way of life.

The main thing is joy is a discipline to be practiced. The Bible says joy is a gift of the Holy Spirit. God says we are to rejoice, and Paul tells us to offer "a sacrifice of praise" (Hebrews 13:15).

For me, the Apostle Paul sums it up best of all in 1 Thessalonians 5:16–23:

> Rejoice evermore.
> Pray without ceasing.
> In every thing give thanks: for this is the will of God in Christ Jesus concerning you.
> Quench not the Spirit.
> Despise not prophesyings.
> Prove all things; hold fast that which is good.
> Abstain from all appearance of evil.
> And the very God of peace sanctify you wholly; and I pray God your whole spirit and soul and body be preserved blameless unto the coming of our Lord Jesus Christ.

12
Running the Good Race

JUST THINK of the Christians you know who are really on fire for the Lord. Now imagine their output and their increased capacity for work and witnessing—if they were in decent physical shape.

I've received numerous letters from Christians like these, asking for advice. I believe God is convicting more and more of us about poor stewardship—whether it be poor time or money management, or negligence of our physical selves.

Are you up to par? How about your family? Does your health do credit to Jesus? What about your physical appearance? Your energy level? What if someone promised you a way to achieve twice as much energy as you now have; would you take it?

Apparently many Christians are asking themselves these questions. Anita and I certainly don't pretend to have all the answers, nor do we dispense advice, but I would like to share the good news about the results obtained so far in our family. Briefly, if Anita and I could think of some way to influence you to begin an exercise program, we would. The benefits our family already knows about literally represent the best news we've found since our salvation.

We're talking about radical changes in you and in your life—at a cost to you of only about twenty minutes a day. Devote those twenty minutes to exercise—and I don't mean housework. The housework a gal does during the day means almost nothing so far as physical fitness and aerobics are concerned.

But for building your endurance and breathing capacity you need to devote that twenty minutes. They will be the most productive, life-inspiring moments of your day and your life. It's pleasurable.

How many calories do you burn in a day? The chart gives the number of calories used during an hour of each sport or activity for your approximate weight.

Sport or activity	125 lbs.	150 lbs.	185 lbs.
Swimming	1241	1291	1359
Running in Place	1221	1479	1821
Jogging	537	651	802
Hiking	488	501	728
Skiing	483	585	721
Tennis	347	420	517
Gardening	295	357	439
Golf	271	328	405
Bicycling	251	304	374
Calisthenics	251	304	374
Dressing or Showering	160	193	238
Office Work	150	181	224
Driving	150	181	224
Sleeping	59	71	88

Some people enjoy the running, but I enjoy the end result of running. People shouldn't say, "I ran twenty minutes and

I hate it." So what? You can manage to sit in the dentist's office that long or longer because it's necessary. So just do it. Do it and get it over with, take a shower, and feel great the rest of the day.

Our family adopted an aerobics program, which has become the most popular physical fitness method throughout the country. Aerobics, developed by Dr. Kenneth H. Cooper, is the official physical fitness program of the U.S. Air Force and the U.S. Navy, and it also has been adopted by the Royal Canadian Air Force.

Today an increasing number of people in the forty to sixty age group have taken up the program, which briefly, includes a variety of exercises that stimulate the heart and lungs long enough to produce beneficial changes in the body. You can choose from among several aerobic exercises —running, swimming, cycling, walking—plus many others. Do whatever turns you on, so long as it forces plenty of oxygen into your system.

Dr. Cooper's book, *The New Aerobics,* started me off. This handy, best-selling paperback explains the whole thing. Almost any newsstand carries it. When you read it— prayerfully, I hope—you'll understand that whatever your age, you can improve your heart, lungs, and vascular system.

The next step will be to commit yourself, because it has to become a way of life. The name of the game is making up your mind, deciding, then not going back on your promise to yourself. If you really want to change yourself physically and think you don't have enough willpower, ask your husband or wife to back you up with prayer. Better still, covenant with one another to try aerobics for one month— together.

Your example will involve your kids too—and I guarantee it. You won't have to nag them. They'll voluntarily join in.

Bobby and I run fifty or sixty minutes out from the house these days, trying to add a new house or landmark every day. The kids enjoy meeting new kitties or dogs or seeing new children. And since we run just before supper time during the summer, the kids have developed a game of trying to decide the nationality of the people who reside in each house, from the food aromas drifting out. They identify spaghetti or Burger King or whatever. During the school year, Bobby and I get up at five o'clock which gives Bobby plenty of time to run, shower, and dress before breakfast at seven o'clock.

I tell Bobby and Gloria that in future years they'll look back and be pleased I started them in this, even if I never influence them in any other way. They'll feel good and feel good about themselves when they are my age. They're starting now to turn themselves into terrific adults.

One curious effect I found in jogging is that although I've always been extremely neat, almost to a fetish, I notice now I'm more apt to take things easy. There's less stress within me.

It's not that I'm getting sloppy, but I don't carry preciseness to an extreme. Most doctors tell you the overprecise people often get into serious stress problems later in life.

As we handled our rough Fourth of July schedule this year, Anita and I discovered how much our conditioning helped us handle the stress—especially Anita.

Because of her relationship to Jesus Christ, Anita is free from much of the stress some other performers experience.

When we work with other big-name stars, I notice that Anita, because of her walk with the Lord, seems much calmer and that her personal life is free from the stress and strife many others seem to experience.

She can calmly concentrate on her performance. She learns song lyrics easily, enjoys her own performances, and seems to maintain a high-energy level in a way non-Christian performers seem to envy.

Mental stress drains energy. If a baseball pitcher, no matter what his physical condition, has personal problems, he finds they drain physical energy from him. He can go out on the mound feeling tired and unfit, regardless of his physical training.

Most people think they can run when they feel like it. The exact opposite is true. It's fine to run (or whatever workout you choose) when you feel good, but the time to run is when you get up tired and don't feel peppy. That's when you run in order to wake up.

Anita formerly didn't really function before noon. She just went through the motions. Such people ought to exercise first thing in the morning and see how much better they feel. I get up in the morning and stagger down, open the garage door, and run out into the street. I know that within one hundred feet of a certain house along my path, I'll suddenly become alert. It's like turning on a light.

At that point the circulation has started, and I'm awake! The most dramatic benefits of all come when you run when you feel terrible. Anita is the first to admit that!

On road trips when I'm really tired, I go out and run and get renewed energy. When we get in late from a road trip—and sometimes it's pretty late at night—I know I'm going to feel lousy when morning comes, but I run anyhow. I feel tired, but the increased blood circulation and oxygen makes body, muscles, and brain work better. That night I make certain I catch up on my sleep.

We don't run every day, but we do try to run five or six days consecutively. Then if we're off for a day or two, we notice all the stored up energy we have—like money in the bank.

When you do knock off one day to attend an important meeting or do some heavy work, you feel that energy surging through you. You feel on top of everything. You feel super-ready for whatever lies ahead of you.

It's a way of life. It's a discipline as firm as my prayer commitment. This type of hard exercise represents self-denial and sacrifice—even at just twenty minutes a day—and God honors that.

If God is speaking to you about yourself or your family, I hope you'll seek His face this minute. Jesus said the fields are ripe to harvest, but the laborers are few (*see* Matthew 9:37, Luke 10:2). The question is are we in any shape to labor?

13
Farfar Goes Home

THE PHONE call came at half-past seven the morning of August 4; Farfar was gone.

"Praise the Lord," I told our doctor. "He's with Jesus."

Dr. Jonas's voice sounded warm and caring. "I'm glad you feel this way. I always dread calling with bad news."

"No, it's good news. Farfar had suffered, but after he came to know Jesus, he prayed to go home. Dr. Jonas, I knew he'd go home today."

"How did you know?"

"A few weeks ago I woke up at four in the morning," I explained. "The Lord seemed to speak to my heart, and He told me Farfar would die on August 4."

I recalled the episode clearly. I supposed the idea sprang from my own mind, that I was projecting and maybe even wanting to get Farfar's ordeal over with. I questioned whether it really was the Lord. But I told Bob about it, and he even told a couple of our close friends.

Later, as the idea returned, I wondered why August 4? Then I counted back and realized that would be five months to the day that Farfar received his salvation. And *that* day had been exactly two years from the day Teddy Heard went to be with the Lord.

The number five in the Bible always represents God's grace. Alvin Dark wore the number five as a ball player. When I sang for a World Series game in 1973, I told Charlie Finley that Oakland would win by God's grace. They won by a score of three to two.

Now I rushed upstairs to Bob. "Dr. Jonas just called, and Farfar is with Jesus," I told him.

"I figured that's what the call was," he said.

Then he began to dress, very deliberately, saying nothing and exhibiting no emotion whatever. I sat and fidgeted, marveling at how long he was taking. At last I said, "Bob, why don't you call Farmor?"

"I'm figuring out how to tell her."

"You don't have to worry," I said. "She's prepared."

And then, for the first time, I got some small reaction. He turned and shot me that warning look that lets me know I'm nagging, but his words were quiet. He simply said, "Anita, let me do it my way."

I didn't understand Bob. In my own big, sprawling family, whenever there is death or other emergency, everyone comes together. People come from all directions, traveling in all sorts of ways, and there's a full range of emotions expressed.

Bob, like his parents, contains most of his emotions. He dreads and fears the possibility that someone will see into him, whereas I customarily let it all hang out.

So I kept waiting for Bob to react as I would react in this situation. The longer he continued calm and slow and quiet, the more it bothered me. And then, just as I thought I would burst, God helped me see the truth. Bob never had experienced the death of a family member before. He had no experience whatever with death, whereas I had much training from watching my older relatives react.

And suddenly I understood many things that had puzzled me then—for example, why Bob, who is so faithful, had become more and more reluctant to visit his dad in the hospital during his last days. I would have stayed around the clock!

How many times Bob has lent me his strength when I needed it, I thought. *And when for the first time he perhaps needed to lean on me—why, I didn't recognize the need.*

A flood of love swept over me then. I understood yet another time how important it is to accept and love your husband even in those ways you don't understand him. And I understood how important it is, not to judge.

During the last days, as Farfar deteriorated rapidly, I spent as many hours as I could beside his bed. I asked Farmor to teach me to say I love you in Swedish, and I said this to him every day. Many days when he lay semiconscious, I read portions of the Bible to him, especially Psalm 91, the Christian's "life insurance policy," which I thought he would understand in the Living Bible version. We also took Gloria and Bobby to see Farfar and let them read Bible verses to him.

As August 4 approached, I asked the florist to make up a special bouquet for Farfar's spiritual birthday. We were not sure how well his eyes functioned, so I ordered something bright. Our florist used bright pink roses, red carnations, and white baby's breath.

I took the bouquet to Farfar, singing "Happy Birthday" and explained why. I wrote on the card:

To our beloved Pop and Farfar, to celebrate your spiritual birthday—from March 4 to August 4, you are five months old. God loves you, and we love you.

I stayed for an hour, but there was virtually no response. I supposed he didn't know I was there, but when I walked to the other side of his bed, he turned his head toward me. Bob and Bobby went over to see Farfar later that evening.

Bob's main concern about Farfar's graduation day seemed to be that there must be no fuss to keep with Farmor's wishes. It had to be quiet. The body was cremated and we had only a short memorial service held at the Northwest Baptist Church with only a few family members in attendance.

As out-of-town friends phoned, offering to fly in, Bob gratefully declined, explaining the brevity of the services as planned, and suggesting that such dear friends as Bruce Howe come later, when there would be time for a visit. They understood.

The more I realized Bob longed for simplicity, the more I wondered what to do. At last I took my courage in hand and said, "If you would like me to, I would be very happy to sing."

"I would like that very much," he said.

"What about Farmor? Would that bother her?"

"I think she would be pleased," Bob told me. "And even if she weren't, she will feel good about it later."

Wednesday, the day Farfar went to be with the Lord,

Bob simply went about his business, it seemed to me. I tried to help by phoning a number of out-of-town friends.

When I phoned our friend Charlotte Allen in Atlanta, I expressed my worry that Bob wouldn't let himself express grief. "He thinks it's unmanly or something, I guess," I told her. "Or maybe that it's unchristian. I'm at a loss to figure it out."

"Expressing emotion is not natural for some people," she told me. "I don't think you should worry, but maybe the Lord is giving you an opportunity to help teach your husband what others have taught you.

"And if he really thinks it's not okay to weep or break down, Jesus did set a precedent. Read John 11:35. Jesus expressed a full range of human emotions."

Thursday evening, we took the children to the mortuary to view their grandfather's earthly shell. He looked so good. Before, when Farfar would come to our house for a party, all dressed up in a nice suit and a bow tie, Bob would inspect him. "Here, let's get you up-to-date, Farfar," he'd say. And he'd go get him a bigger bow tie.

When we walked in the chapel and I noticed the dark blue bow tie Bob had chosen, I had a little chuckle—"Even now, Bob is still dressing Farfar. And he *does* look handsome."

I had just read a remarkable book, one which had such impact on me. In *What Is a Family?*, Edith Schaeffer, the noted American author and lecturer who lives in L'Abri, Switzerland, talks about building a library of memories.

I realized that for our children, and for us, this evening was something real and something strong, a time we will remember, each in our own way. I watched as the two younger ones approached Farfar's casket.

"That's not Farfar," Barbara said. "He's in heaven."

Billy said, "Can I touch him?" I said, "Surely." So he did, and then he said, "Boy, is he cold!"

I felt really embarrassed. The kids seemed so matter-of-fact. They literally accepted that Farfar had gone to heaven, and shed no tears whatever. I began to wonder if their reactions were wrong.

And then Brother Bill Chapman came in. We had been out of town so much in recent weeks that this became a real reunion. Bob hugged him, and then I did. When I found a moment to speak of the children's odd reactions, he reassured me.

"That's good," he said. "They're curious and factual, but not disrespectful. The wonderful thing is they know he is with Jesus."

Then he prayed a sweet prayer, and we all said good-bye to that part of Farfar that we could see. We spoke of the Resurrection; and Farmor cried.

Then we went to dinner. We all talked freely about Farfar, remarking how much he enjoyed eating. I said, "As good as this food is, imagine the feast he's having with Jesus. Imagine him seeing Grandma and Grandpa Berry, Teddy Heard, and Dan Topping, meeting Aunt Berthie for the first time, and all the Apostles, and learning all the answers to life. What a wonderful feast for Farfar!"

And so it went, all talking in a very spirited, lively, happy way.

Wednesday evening, only hours after Farfar's death, Bob and Bobby jogged four miles. I still worried about Bob's unexpressed grief. Then I realized he was working it off through his physical body. I thanked God for the release running gives Bob.

Just before Farfar's services, I lost the victory. Trying to get the kids all dressed, trying to tidy up the house a little, and running and scurrying, I happened to discover the twins had messed up the nursery. For one thing, Billy had concocted some sort of pudding, which I only discovered after getting it on my dress.

I was furious. I yelled at him at the top of my lungs and smacked his bottom hard—meanwhile, saying a prayer that I wouldn't spank him at such a time.

So we departed for the church in a somewhat unsettled and inharmonious state. I felt very annoyed at myself, and also very ill at ease over how Farmor would react when I sang. I knew she didn't want to get emotional, and I knew she didn't believe Farfar was saved. More and more, my singing seemed like a bad idea. Although we had told her it was unnecessary, Gloria Roe Robertson decided to fly in and agreed to play for me.

The service was simple, as Bob had wanted, and also strong and dignified, like Farfar. He would have liked the plain, solid oak casket Bob chose. Because Farfar had been a carpenter, he would have appreciated the hand carving and the good construction.

The friends who had prayed for Farfar—Charlie and Fredda Walker, Charlie Morgan, Chuck and Hope Bird, Dick and Ruth Shack, Alvin and Jackie Dark, and so many other precious church friends were there. One person came to represent one of my former Sunday school girls who couldn't be there. When Sandy Ferguson's mother died, I attended her funeral. Now little Sandy was remembering and wanting to honor Farfar. I thought that was sweet.

And Dr. Stanley Jonas was there. How can such a busy doctor clear his calendar and come be with us on a Friday afternoon, I wondered. It was a blessing to have the funeral arrangements made by Brother Alex Stamey who was with the funeral home and made sure everything was done in a Christian and professional manner.

I sang "How Great Thou Art." It's such a magnificent hymn, so powerful, and for Farfar, so appropriate. It is a Scandinavian hymn, after all.

It was very fitting to sing all three inspiring verses—including the one I used to omit:

And when I think that God, his Son not sparing,
Sent him to die, I scarce can take it in;
That on the cross, my burden gladly bearing,
He bled and died to take away my sin.

God was faithful to give me the strength and the power. That great song ministered to me then, as it always does.

Later, as we rode home in the limousine, Farmor said, "I was surprised when you sang. I didn't think you would when I heard you yelling at the children."

"Farmor, you know I am only too human," I said. "Unfortunately!"

Farmor frequently has to tell her friends that I am too busy to sing for all the requests that are made. She seemed to think it might have been an imposition to ask me to sing at the service.

Then I loved on Billy and asked him to forgive me for getting so upset with him. I try to punish the children in love, never when I'm upset or angry.

At the request of Farmor, Brother Claude Wilson, our associate pastor, spoke with a victorious assurance, his words filled with the Gospel. Brother Wilson had impressed Farmor when he visited Farfar in the hospital. His strength and warmth inspires us all. Our pastor, Brother Bill Chapman, had opened the service with a Scripture and prayer.

"Just five months ago, this precious man accepted Jesus Christ as his Lord and Savior. I found Mr. Green to be a very honest man, and I love honesty. I believe when Mr. Green told us something, it was absolutely, 100 percent true. This honesty was so meaningful when Mr. Green said he trusted the Lord as his Savior, because had he not been as honest, he would not have said it. And because he did say it, he did mean it. And this is precious. . . ."

Brother Wilson read Psalm 27:13–14:

I had fainted, unless I had believed to see the goodness of the LORD in the land of the living.

Wait on the LORD: be of good courage, and he shall strengthen thine heart: wait, I say, on the LORD.

He told us the good news about believing, and we rejoiced that Farfar believed. We left with love and peace and joy in our hearts, happy to leave Farfar in the arms of his Father.

And then we were going home. Home to Villa Verde,

home to rest and perhaps quiet, although you never know.

And I thought of all the unanswered questions, the perplexities of those few days, and I wondered that they seemed to have melted away.

"You don't need to understand, Anita," the Lord seemed to say. "Just accept." And I thought of all there is to learn about my own husband and myself, about Farmor and the children, much less all the others in our world.

Edith Schaeffer had expressed it so beautifully, I thought: the fact that your family is, in microcosm, the Body of Christ. Each supplies what another lacks. Anita weeps but sings . . . Bob becomes quiet, yet hosts a family dinner . . . Billy touches . . . Barbara and Gloria clean up the house . . . Bobby runs beside his father. . . .

And now I realize, even though imperfectly, what we are running toward. Running the good race will bring us, when the Lord wills, into His own shining, perfect presence.

And as the automobile glided quietly toward Villa Verde, I rejoiced for Farfar, already with the Lord. The sunlight glancing off the children's blond heads seemed dazzling, and the Scripture Brother Bill had just read returned to my mind:

Who shall separate us from the love of Christ? shall tribulation, or distress, or persecution, or famine, or nakedness, or peril, or sword?

As it is written, For thy sake we are killed all the day long; we are accounted as sheep for the slaughter.

Nay, in all these things we are more than conquerors through him that loved us.

For I am persuaded, that neither death, nor life, nor an-

H 23

gels, nor principalities, nor powers, nor things present, nor things to come,

Nor height, nor depth, nor any other creature, shall be able to separate us from the love of God, which is in Christ Jesus our Lord.

Romans 8:35–39

Welcome, Farfar, I thought. *Happy homecoming. We love you!*

And then we, the rest of the Green team, were home, also. The grand old house, accustomed to feet running and puppies barking and a mommie who sometimes yells, just seemed to reach out and draw us in, with a *welcome.*

Praise God!